AN INDIGENOUS PEOPLES' HISTORY OF THE UNITED STATES

FOR YOUNG PEOPLE

AN INDIGENOUS PEOPLES' HISTORY OF THE UNITED STATES

FOR YOUNG PEOPLE

ROXANNE DUNBAR-ORTIZ

ADAPTED BY JEAN MENDOZA AND DEBBIE REESE

BEACON PRESS ■ BOSTON

BEACON PRESS
Boston, Massachusetts
www.beacon.org

Beacon Press books
are published under the auspices of
the Unitarian Universalist Association of Congregations.

25 24 23 22   18 17 16

This book is printed on acid-free paper that meets the uncoated paper
ANSI/NISO specifications for permanence as revised in 1992.

Text design by Carol Chu and Kim Arney
Text composition by Kim Arney

Beacon Press gratefully acknowledges the Wallace Action
Fund of Tides Foundation for their support of this project.

Library of Congress Cataloging-in-Publication Data
Names: Mendoza, Jean, author. | Reese, Debbie, author. | Adaptation of
     (work): Dunbar-Ortiz, Roxanne ; Indigenous peoples' history of the
     United States.
Title: An indigenous peoples' history of the United States for young
     people / Roxanne Dunbar-Ortiz ; adapted by Jean Mendoza and
     Debbie Reese.
Description: Boston : Beacon Press, [2019] | Includes bibliographical
     references and index.
Identifiers: LCCN 2019004266 (print) | LCCN 2019017710 (ebook) |
     ISBN 9780807049402 (ebook) | ISBN 9780807049396 (pbk. : alk. paper)
Subjects: LCSH: Indians of North America—Historiography—Juvenile
     literature. | Indians of North America—Colonization—Juvenile literature. |
     Indians, Treatment of—United States—History—Juvenile literature. |
     United States—Colonization—Juvenile literature. | United States—Race
     relations—Juvenile literature. | United States—Politics and government—
     Juvenile literature.
Classification: LCC E76.8 (ebook) | LCC E76.8 .R44 2019 (print) |
     DDC 970.004/97—dc23
LC record available at https://lccn.loc.gov/2019004266

CONTENTS

Indigenous? American Indian! Or . . . Native American?!

You may have heard people use these three different terms to refer to the peoples that are the focus of this book. All three are correct, depending on whom you ask. The three terms are also used interchangeably by federal, state, and tribal governments. The most accurate term anyone can use is the specific name of the nation that you are talking about. Throughout this book we will use specific names, and when we are making a point about two or more nations, we will use one of the broader terms.

One term you've probably heard most often in TV shows, movies, and stories to talk about groups of Native people is *tribe*. The word *nation* is more accurate than the word *tribe* because it acknowledges that long before the United States existed, the many different Native peoples had governments and made agreements with each other, just as other nations have always done. The US government and tribal governments also use the terms *tribe* and *nation* interchangeably. Some Native nations include the word *tribe* in their names, as you'll see in the final chapter about the Standing Rock Sioux Tribe. Others use the word *band*, and still others use *rancheria*.

Those television shows, movies, and stories rarely, if ever, provide useful information about the number of people in any given nation. Some nations were, and are, quite large, while some are smaller. Today, the Cherokee Nation has about 260,000 tribal citizens living across the

United States, and there are currently 1,900 Taos Indians living on Taos Pueblo lands.

In addition to the interchangeable phrases and the different uses of *nation* and *tribe*, the different nations use different words for themselves! Some use *tribal member* and some use *tribal citizen*. You would be correct in saying, "Debbie Reese is a tribal member of Nambé Pueblo," and you would be correct in saying that "Wilma Mankiller was a citizen of the Cherokee Nation."

That sounds like a lot, but there's even more! For example, the word *Inuit* means "people" in their language. So, to someone who speaks that language, "the Inuit people" is redundant because that phrase ultimately means "the people people." And on top of that, tribal nations are turning to their own names for themselves. The people previously called the Winnebago are actually the Ho-Chunk. In recent years, maps and other printed materials have been changed to reflect a tribal nation's preference to be known by their own name for themselves.

You will see that often when we refer to geographic locations such as states, we use phrases like "currently known as." One reason we do that is to make clear that many present-day boundaries and names would have been meaningless to the Indigenous people during the time covered in a chapter. Another reason is that names can be, and often are, changed in response to events or to requests from Native communities. In 2008, for example, "Squaw Peak," in what is currently known as Arizona, was renamed. Native people had long objected to the name. The word *squaw* is loosely based on an Algonquian term but was used by settlers in a way that degraded Native women. After Lori Piestewa, a Hopi soldier, was killed in the Iraq War, the peak was renamed in her honor.

In short, naming is in a constant state of change! Some names in this book may have gone out of use by the time the book is sent from the publisher to your home or classroom. These are good changes, though, because they are evidence that Indigenous knowledges are becoming more widely embraced. Later printings of this book will likely incorporate more language changes that happen.

There's a lot to consider here, and we hope that this introduction to names and words helps you as you read through this book.

Some of you will be surprised at our references to slavery. We took care to refer to people as "enslaved" rather than as "slaves" because the word "slaves" turns people into objects, and that is a violation of their humanity. And some of you may be surprised to read the passages about Native slavery and enslavement. Most history books do not say that Native people were sometimes enslaved and that some Native people used enslaved labor, but that is part of the history that we all need to learn. In the coming years, we hope that it will become common knowledge.

One more thing to know! For a long time, textbooks and other print media have put non-English words in italics. Setting words apart in that way signals that English is the normal way to speak and write and other languages are "different." But many people now see this use of italics as a way of "othering" languages and the people who speak them. We are strong advocates for the shift away from italics. You will not see Native words in italics in this book.

THIS LAND

Under the crust of that part of the earth called the United States of America are buried the bones, villages, fields, and sacred objects of the first people of that land—the people who are often called American Indians or Native Americans. Their descendants, also called Indigenous peoples, carry memories and stories of how the United States came to be the nation we know today. It is important to learn and know this history, but many people today lack that knowledge and understanding because of the way America's story has been taught.

Like most people, Americans want to think well of themselves, their ancestors, their history, and what they and their leaders do. As advanced technology makes the experiences of Indigenous peoples around the world more readily available, it is necessary that Americans learn to think more completely and more critically about their own history, because it can help them be better citizens of the world. Part of that critical thinking involves recognition that "America" is a name given to two land masses by European colonizers. Indigenous peoples had, and have, words for the land in their own languages.

■ THEN AND NOW

Everything in US history is about the land: who oversaw it and planted crops on it, fished its waters, maintained

its wildlife; who invaded and stole it; how it became
a commodity ("real estate") broken into pieces to be
bought and sold. As anthropologist Patrick Wolfe writes,
"Land is life—or at least, land is necessary for life."[1]

One interesting activity is to quickly draw a rough
outline of the US at the time it gained independence from
Britain. Go ahead—take out a sheet of paper and try it!

▪ Did your outline look something like this?

▪ Or did it look more like this?

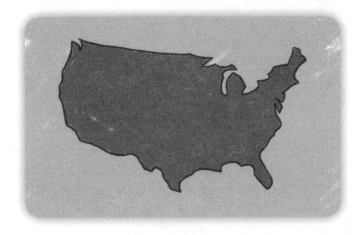

Teachers who have done this activity with their students say that most of them draw the shape of the current United States from the Atlantic to the Pacific. But the US didn't look like that until a century after independence. What became independent in 1783 were just thirteen British colonies hugging the Atlantic shore.

When teachers remind students of this, they are embarrassed. They know better, but somehow they forget! They are not alone. This is a common mistake.

What has happened since Europeans first encountered the land masses known as North and South America? Most books about American history say they were discovered by Christopher Columbus and other Europeans, settled by courageous English citizens seeking religious freedom, and expanded by brave settlers who moved westward in search of adventure and a better life. Most people's understanding of what it means to be an

American is founded upon such tales, which together form a myth-like origin story.

ORIGIN STORIES OF THE UNITED STATES

Origin narratives, or "stories about how this all began," help a group of people feel that they belong to a community with a common past and shared ideas about what is important. Origin stories are central to a people's sense of a unifying identity. However, origin stories may leave out key aspects of what actually happened and overemphasize others. That is the case with the most familiar origin story of the United States.

In the late fifteenth century, as European explorers sailed to unfamiliar places, their actions and beliefs were guided by the Doctrine of Discovery—the idea that European nations could claim the foreign lands they "discovered." The Doctrine of Discovery was laid out in a series of communications from the pope, leader of the Catholic Church, who was extremely influential in European politics at the time. It asserted that Indigenous inhabitants lost their natural right to that land as soon as Europeans arrived and claimed it. People whose homelands were "discovered" were considered subjects of the Europeans and were expected to do what the "discoverers" wished. If they resisted, they were to be conquered by European military action. This enabled Columbus to claim the Taíno people's Caribbean home for Spain and to kidnap and enslave the Indigenous peoples. Similarly, the Pilgrims and the Puritans, the first groups from England to settle what became the United States, believed they had a covenant with God to take the land. The Doctrine

Landing of Columbus, by painter John Vanderlyn, is a mural in the Capitol Rotunda in Washington, DC. It is a typical depiction of the 1492 "discovery of America."

of Discovery influenced the policies of the young United States and directly affected the lives and the very existence of Native people. However, history textbooks for young people rarely invite students to question or think critically about that part of the US origin story.

"Free" land, with all its resources, was a magnet that attracted European settlers to the Americas. The word *settler* is used so frequently that most people do not recognize that it means more than just a person who settles down to live in a new place. Throughout history it has also meant a person who goes to live where, supposedly, no one has lived before. More often than not, "settlers" have gone to live somewhere that is already home to someone else. They are important to a nation—like Britain or Spain—when it plans to set up colonies in an area. Colonization is the process of taking political and economic control of a region, and colonizers are the people

Cree artist William Kent Monkman reimagined the "discovery of America" with oddly dressed, ill-mannered, and greedy invaders.

or institutions that are part of that process: the military, business interests, people who go there to live, and sometimes representatives of religious institutions. Because of their key role in establishing and populating a colony, settlers may be called colonizers. Settlers who came to what is currently known as North America wanted land for homes, farms, and businesses that they could not have in their home countries. Settlers who used the labor of enslaved Africans wanted limitless land for growing cash crops. Under their nations' flags, those Europeans fought Native people for control of that land.

Even when the United States consisted of just a few states on the Eastern Seaboard, the country's founders fully intended for "America" to extend "from sea to shining sea." In fact, the first law of the new nation was created because of that demand for land. The Continental Congress wrote the Northwest Ordinance in 1787, two years before the Constitution was ratified. It allowed settlers to live in "Indian Territory" west of the Appalachian and Allegheny Mountains. Before that, the British government's Proclamation of 1763 prohibited settlement there.

The territory affected by the Northwest Ordinance of 1787 included parts of what are currently known as the states of Ohio, Michigan, Indiana, Illinois, Wisconsin, and Minnesota.

In 1801 President Thomas Jefferson described the intent to expand the boundaries of the United States, saying, "It is impossible not to look forward to distant times, when our rapid multiplication will . . . cover the whole northern, if not the southern continent, with a people speaking the same language, governed in similar forms, and by similar laws."[2]

This idea eventually came to be called Manifest Destiny—the belief that English-speaking Americans were destined to spread their presence and their ideals across the entire continent. Manifest Destiny was the banner under which the homelands of Indigenous peoples would be taken.

VIEWS OF US HISTORY

If you read many US history books, you may find several interpretations of the country's origin myth. As later chapters of this book will point out, many interpretations of the origin myth misrepresent and do injustice to peoples indigenous to this land.

For example, many school textbooks uncritically accept the ideas expressed in the Doctrine of Discovery, Jefferson's statement on expansion, and Manifest Destiny. They treat expansion of the US from Atlantic to Pacific as inevitable and good. Whatever stood in the way (that is, Native nations and their citizens) was seen as a problem to be overcome by any means necessary, including military force.

Another interpretation of the US origin myth found in some history books is the idea that relations between the Native people and the European Americans should be viewed as a *cultural conflict*. This view was a reaction against the civil rights movement and student activism of the 1960s and was seen as objective and fair. This view is expressed in statements such as the following:

- "There were good people and bad people on both sides."
- "American culture is an amalgamation of all its ethnic groups."
- "A frontier is a zone of interaction between cultures, not merely advancing European settlements."
- "The Natives and the European Americans experienced an encounter at the frontier and engaged in dialogue."

Some who hold this view even suggest that Indigenous cultures were responsible for their own demise. In trying to be objective and fair, such perspectives ignore centuries of US policy and law that did not question whether European Americans had the right to take over the entire continent.

A *multicultural* interpretation of US history emphasizes only the "contributions" of groups that were ignored in the dominant origin myth, including Indigenous peoples, women, African Americans, and immigrants. Indigenous peoples are portrayed as having helped make the country great by sharing corn, beans, buckskin, log cabins, parkas, maple syrup, canoes, and even the basic concepts of democracy. But the idea that "gifts" from Indians helped to establish and enrich the US hides that these resources were taken, often by force, as the country expanded. The multicultural perspective tends to cast Indigenous peoples in general as an oppressed racial group without considering important political differences between the Native nations and other oppressed populations. It says little or nothing about the theft of Indigenous lands and the cultural destruction that made "unity" possible.

◾ AN INDIGENOUS PERSPECTIVE

Today in the United States there are more than five hundred federally recognized Indigenous nations composed of nearly three million people. These are the descendants of the fifteen million original inhabitants of the land, the majority of whom were farmers who lived in towns.

The Indigenous peoples' land base has also been drastically reduced since first contact with Europeans. Walter R. Echo-Hawk writes that Indian landholdings in the US had plummeted to 156 million acres by 1881. By 1934, about 50 million acres remained. During World War II, the US government took 500,000 more acres for military use.[3]

Much of that remaining land consists of more than three hundred federally recognized reservations. The concept of reservation—confining an Indigenous group to a reserved land base in exchange for US government protection from settlers—arose during the era of US expansion and treaty making that spanned the years from independence to 1871.

Although Native historians and scholars have written at length about how events in US history have impacted Indigenous peoples, their perspectives are not often

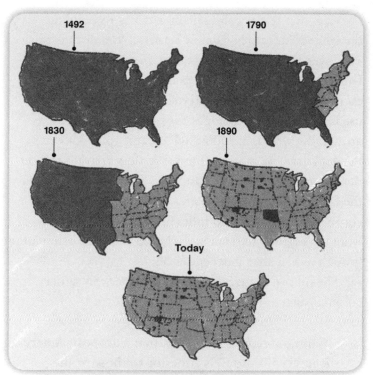

The map dramatically shows the reduction in Indigenous lands, but its scale does not allow the "today" map to accurately depict all existing tribal offices and land holdings across the country.

included in history courses. Instead, students are taught another origin story, one about the US as a nation of immigrants. Native peoples, to the extent that they are included at all, are conveniently renamed "First Americans," which casts them as immigrants (usually from Asia across the Bering Strait), undermining their claims to the land.

The "nation of immigrants" framework obscures the US practice of *settler colonialism*. This book takes the view that settler colonialism was key to building the United States. The goal of settler colonialism is to take over all resources in a region, particularly the land. During the colonial era, for example, European business corporations received military support to take over and use land and other resources for profit in foreign areas around the world, including what came to be known as the Americas. As more and more settlers arrived, one settlement paved the way for another, and another. This gave the European governments and the government-backed corporations control and influence farther and farther from the original settlements. The US followed a similar growth model after independence.

The following ideas are basic to American settler colonialism:

- White supremacy. The idea that European American "civilization" is superior to those of the American Indians and of the Africans who were enslaved for economic gain is called white supremacy. At the individual level, this means that "white" lives are seen as more valuable than those of darker-skinned people.
- African American slavery. Although slavery is mostly associated with the American South, the entire country, as it grew, benefitted from the enslavement of people, primarily Africans and African Americans.
- A policy of genocide and land theft. The United Nations now defines *genocide* as an act, or acts, "committed with intent to destroy, in whole or in

part, a national, ethnical, racial or religious group."[4] These acts are

a. Killing members of the group;
b. Causing serious bodily or mental harm to members of the group;
c. Deliberately inflicting on the group conditions of life calculated to bring about its physical destruction in whole or in part;
d. Imposing measures intended to prevent births within the group;
e. Forcibly transferring children of the group to another group.

The following statement from General William T. Sherman in 1873 is an example of what genocidal attitudes sound like:

> We must act with vindictive earnestness against the Sioux, even to their extermination, men, women and children . . . during an assault, the soldiers can not pause to distinguish between male and female, or even discriminate as to age.[5]

The continued influence of settler colonialism and genocide show up when history is retold in a way that

CONSIDER THIS

Let's consider the word *civilization*. Who decides what *civilization* is? And how does our definition shape how we think about societies and the people in them?

James Earle Fraser's *End of the Trail* was exhibited at the 1915 World's Fair. It is an example of imagery created by non-Native artists that incorrectly suggests Indigenous people had come to the end of their existence and are no longer here.

celebrates settlers and makes Indigenous peoples disappear from the historical record. This practice is sometimes called "firsting and lasting."[6] You may have seen examples of it. All over North America are places that are described as "the first" settlement, building, or school. Invariably this means the first settlement, building, or school created by white settlers, as if no one lived there before they came.

On the other hand, stories of the US are also full of instances of the "last" Indians or last tribes—"the last of the Mohicans," "Ishi, the last Indian," and *End of the Trail* (a famous sculpture created by James Earle Fraser).

Settler colonialism requires violence or the threat of violence to attain its goals. You will read more about the US history of settler colonialism, white supremacy, slavery, genocide, and land theft in later chapters. You will also read of the many ways in which Native nations and communities have fought for their survival. After all, people do not hand over their land, resources, children, and futures without a struggle! Modern Indigenous nations and communities are societies shaped by their resistance to colonialism.

TO DO

Native nations have their own websites, just like the fifty US states do. Go online and study a handful of them. How does the information they provide compare to what you've seen elsewhere about Native people?

■   ■   ■

This book tells the story of the United States as a colonialist settler-state, one that sought to crush and subjugate Indigenous populations. In spite of all that was done to them, Indigenous peoples are still here.

It is breathtaking, but no miracle, that they have survived as peoples.

This is a history of the United States.

CHAPTER ONE

FOLLOW THE CORN

History books often refer to "the New World" to talk about the lands now called North and South America. That term reflects a European perspective. That part of the world was not new to the people who had lived there for thousands of years when the Europeans arrived. It was home.

DID YOU KNOW?

Societies have always had their own ways of marking calendar time. You are probably familiar with the abbreviations BC and AD. BC stands for "Before Christ." "Anno domini" is Latin for "Year of Our Lord" and refers to time since the birth of Jesus. Those terms have special meaning to societies in which Christianity is the dominant religion and are commonly used even in places where it is not. Two other abbreviations that acknowledge Christianity is not everyone's religion are also used in this chapter to respect that other religions, including those of the Indigenous peoples discussed in this chapter, are as important as Christianity. They are BCE (Before the Common Era), and CE (Common Era). This need not be confusing; the year 45 BCE is the same as 45 BC, and the year 1945 CE is the same as AD 1945.

TO DO

Corn is an English word that has been used to describe grain crops including wheat and oats. The scientific name for the "corn" that was cultivated in the Americas is Zea mays. "Mays" comes from the Spanish pronunciation of the Taíno word for this crop: mahiz. In the Ojibwe language the word is mandaamin. As more nations put their languages into apps and websites, you have opportunities to learn words in those languages. Take a look at websites that tribal nations have created. Some have links to pages about their language. See what other words for corn you can find.

Human societies originated in sub-Saharan Africa. About two hundred thousand years ago, the people began migrating out from Africa and around the globe. Around fifteen thousand years ago, they began to occupy seven areas.

Three of the seven areas were on the land masses that are currently called the Americas. They are the Valley of Mexico and Central America (sometimes called Meso-america), the South Central Andes in South America, and eastern North America.

By around 8500 BCE, societies in all seven areas of settlement were domesticating and cultivating plants. In the Americas, the most important plant the Indigenous peoples grew was maize, or corn.

CORN: A SACRED FOOD

Prior to 1492 corn did not exist outside the Americas. Scientists have evidence that Indigenous peoples in

Central Mexico cultivated corn ten thousand years ago, around 8000 BCE.

Twelve to fourteen centuries later (6800–6600 BCE), corn production had spread from the central valley south to the tip of South America, north to the subarctic, and to both coasts of the two continents. This proliferation of corn and other crops such as beans, squash, and potatoes required vast networks of cultural and commercial exchange among the peoples of North, Central, and South America.

Thousands of years ago Indigenous scientists turned a wild grain into a food source that sustained their bodies and their spiritual lives. Unlike other grains, corn cannot grow wild. Without attentive care from Indigenous peoples, it would not exist. The people of Central America cultivated corn in many colors. It was even grown in deserts and other areas that were very dry. Growing it there required complex irrigation systems.

By the end of the 1500s CE, the total population of what we now call the Western Hemisphere was about one hundred million people. Approximately forty million were in North America and Mexico. Central Mexico alone supported some thirty million people. For comparison, at that time the population of all Europe extending to the Ural Mountains in Eastern Russia was about seventy million.

Scientists attribute the significantly larger population in the Americas to a relatively disease-free society whose use of herbal medicine, surgery, dentistry, and hygienic and ritual bathing kept disease at bay.

Let's take a look at people and corn in the area that is now Mexico and Central America.

CONSIDER THIS

In elementary school, did you learn that some Indigenous peoples thought of corn, beans, and squash as "the three sisters"? Did you help plant a "three sisters" garden as a school project?

Have you read a story about the Three Sisters? Do you know the source of that story? Do you know what Native nation it belongs to?

Those questions are important ones. It is true that Native communities all across the North American continent grew those three crops and told stories about them. They still do. But it is also true that Native stories were appropriated (taken and used without permission) in ways that distort what they mean to the Native nation they belong to. It might surprise you to learn that many stories of how the "three sisters" came to be aren't Native stories at all! They might look like Native stories, but they were made up by people who are not Native.

Learning to ask questions about who tells a history, or a story, is an important goal of this book. What you read shapes how you think about the world, whether it is history or story. And it shapes how you look at, and think about, people in the world too.

THE ORIGINS OF CORN IN MEXICO AND CENTRAL AMERICA

What we know today as Mexico and Central America are vast areas of land where many different nations of people lived, and have lived, for thousands of years. You can probably remember hearing about the Mayans and the Aztecs, but throughout the history of that region peoples of many distinct nations were living side by side, sometimes trading with each other, sometimes at war with each other, sometimes absorbing or conquering one another.

In addition to the Mayan and Aztec civilizations, the Olmec, Toltec, and Culhua peoples thrived in Mesoamerica at different times. So did others, such as the Tepanec, Texcoco, and Tlacopan. Some of these peoples conquered others. Many were then conquered by the Aztecs who had migrated from northern Mexico.

Conquered, or conqueror, they all had one thing in common: they cultivated corn.

The first great cultivators of corn were the Mayans. Their civilization was initially centered in what is now northern Guatemala and in Tabasco, a state in present-day Mexico. In fact, the cultivation of corn was at the core of Mayan culture. Their religion centered around this vital food.

The Mayans of the tenth century CE built city-states as far south as Belize and Honduras. Today, those who study Mayan culture are astonished by their art, architecture, sculpture, and painting and their understandings of time and mathematics. By 36 BCE they had developed the concept of zero and sophisticated calendar systems. They studied the movements of the moon and planets and predicted eclipses.

DEFINITION

A *city-state* is an independent state or nation consisting of a city and its surrounding territory.

The Mayan people were governed by a system in which the priesthood and the nobility shared the power to make and enforce laws that affected all of Mayan society. War prisoners, criminals, debtors, and orphans could be forced into labor. Mayans who lived away from the cities worked the nobles' fields and paid rent to use the land for their own needs. Their labor and their taxes helped to build roads, temples, nobles' houses, and other structures. We do not know if they were content with this arrangement or if they felt exploited. Mayan dominance of the region lasted more than five hundred years. Eventually dissension and uprisings led to the collapse of the Mayan state. The end of their political power in the region did not mean the end of the Mayans themselves. Contemporary Mayan people live today throughout the lands of their ancestors.

At the same time that Mayan civilization was developing, the Olmecs, sometimes called Mexico's "Mother Culture," flourished in the Valley of Mexico. The Toltec, Culhua, and Tepanec cultures subsequently dominated (and sometimes struggled for dominance) in that region. Meanwhile, the Aztecs extended their influence in the valley and eventually consolidated their power. By 1426 CE, they and their allies had overthrown the Tepanecs, and they soon moved to bring all the peoples of Mexico under their authority.

The economic basis for the powerful Aztec state was hydraulic agriculture. Corn was their most important crop, but beans, pumpkins, tomatoes, cocoa, and other food crops flourished and supported the dense population. They also grew tobacco and cotton.

Weaving and metalwork were valued as works of art. Along with the crops, they were useful commodities in the marketplaces of each city in the trade networks initially established by the Toltecs.

These networks reached into what we know today as the Southwest and West Coast of the United States. Turquoise, macaw and parrot feathers, seashells, obsidian, flint, and animal hides were among the many items traded among all the peoples who were part of this trade network.

The Aztecs flourished culturally, economically, militarily, and politically, but they faced growing rebellion by the peoples from whom they exacted tribute. Tribute is payment of some kind that a ruler demands of peoples who have been conquered. The Aztecs required tribute in the form of military service, physical labor, crops, and manufactured products.

The Spanish conquistador Cortez recruited the rebels as allies, making it possible for the Spanish to crush Mexico and level its cities in a three-year genocidal war. Though the Aztecs lost control of Mexico, like the Mayans their descendants are part of today's societies in Mexico and the US.

Let's turn now to corn in the area of the continent that we know today as the United States.

CORN IN THE NORTH

The area known today as the southwestern United States was once the northern periphery of the Aztec empire. Most of it is a fragile land base where the elevation is high, rainfall is scarce, and drought is a part of life. And yet, by 2100 BCE, the Hohokam peoples of that area had traded for, and were cultivating, corn, beans, squash, and cotton. Among their descendants are the Akimel O'Odham. They built one of the most extensive networks of irrigation canals in the world at that time. The largest canals were seventy-five to eighty feet across and twenty feet deep. Many of them were lined with clay, which made them leakproof. A single canal system could carry enough water to irrigate an estimated ten thousand acres.

From the Atlantic Ocean to the Mississippi River, and south from the Great Lakes to the Gulf of Mexico was one of the most fertile agricultural belts in the world. In the twelfth century CE, the Mississippi Valley region was home to several large city-states that were built of earthen stepped pyramids much like those in Mexico. The largest of these was Cahokia. Cahokia supported a population of tens of thousands, larger than that of London during that same time period. The scale of their constructions and their agriculture infrastructure required sophisticated civic and social organization. One of the mounds at Cahokia is believe to be the largest earthwork in the Americas to have been built before the European invasions.

The people of these "mound builder" civilizations dispersed before the European invasion, but we know their descendants today as the Cherokee, Chickasaw, Choctaw, Muscogee Creek, and Natchez Nations of the Southeast. These tribes retained some of the political complexity of the Cahokian culture. Their tribal governments had three branches: a civil administration, a military, and a

This mound at Cahokia is about 98 feet tall and covers 14 acres (approximately the size of fourteen football fields). It is currently named Monks Mound after some Catholic monks who lived on or near it in the 1800s. Perhaps one day it will be renamed by Native people whose ancestors lived at Cahokia.

branch that dealt with the sacred. Autonomous tribal towns made decisions about trade and relations with other groups, but in some political and social matters, the towns worked together as a confederacy to make decisions that affected all of their members.

These southeastern peoples and their descendants today maintain important traditions related to corn, such as Green Corn ceremonies.

The Haudenosaunee Confederacy, sometimes referred to as the Six Nations of the Iroquois Confederacy, developed in what is now the northeastern part of the United States. It was made up of the Seneca, Cayuga, Onondaga, Oneida, and Mohawk Nations and was later joined by the Tuscaroras. This confederacy incorporated six widely dispersed nations comprising thousands of agricultural villages and hunting grounds in what are currently known as New York, Pennsylvania, and Quebec. By collective stewardship of the land and a clan-village system of democracy it avoided giving all the political control and decision-making to a single group. Corn, their staple crop, was stored in granaries and distributed equitably by clan mothers, the oldest woman from each extended family. In this confederacy, the clan mothers also played a key role in governance. They chose the men who would represent their clans in the governing councils, and they held the power to recall unsatisfactory representatives. They also had the right to speak in the council.

The Haudenosaunee people today retain a fully functioning confederacy, similar to what they had before European arrival. The Haudenosaunee Constitution, called the Great Law of Peace, inspired some key parts of the US Constitution.

No matter where they were, Indigenous peoples' governance was based on valuing what was best for the community over the needs or preferences of individuals.

Indigenous peoples sustained their populations not only by adapting to their specific natural environments but also by changing their environments to meet their needs. This is regarded as stewardship, or being stewards of the land. A steward is someone who is responsible for the purposeful, careful management of resources so that the needs of a group can be met, both in the present and in the future. Someone who exploits the resources for gain only in the present, leaving them ruined for future use, would not be considered a steward.

By the time the European invasions began, Indigenous peoples had occupied and made changes to every part of the Americas.

Let's take a quick look at two of the ways Indigenous peoples managed their lands and resources prior to European invasion. We will specifically consider the use of fire for agriculture and game management, and the creation of roadways that spanned the continent.

One main tool for shaping nature was fire. Indigenous communities regularly used fire in multiple ways that changed the precolonial North American landscape. For example, Indigenous farmers of the Northeast always carried flints to start fires as needed. Such controlled fires helped to clear space in the forest for growing corn and other crops. Instead of the densely wooded wilderness Europeans depicted in literature and art, the real American landscape included cornfields, berry patches, and groves of nut trees that contributed to the food supply.

They used fire to clear space for other purposes too. Most Indigenous peoples of the Americas, unlike the people of Europe, Africa, and Asia, did not domesticate animals for a ready supply of hides and meat. Instead they created havens to attract elk, deer, bear, and other game for hunting. One strategy for doing this was to burn the undergrowth in forests. In the following springtime animals were drawn to the young plants that sprouted. Hunters killed what the community needed to replenish supplies of meat and hides.

The Indigenous peoples who lived on the Great Plains also used fire to extend those vast grasslands to make more grazing lands for buffalo herds. With parts of the forest cleared by fire, the herds could roam the East. Native peoples also left an indelible imprint on the land with systems of roads that tied their nations and communities together across the entire landmass of the Americas. These were not just hunting paths that followed game trails or routes that peoples could easily follow during seasonal migrations. They were well-traveled roads that tracked major rivers, like the Mississippi, Ohio, Missouri, Columbia, Colorado, and the Rio Grande. Some followed seacoasts. One ran along the Pacific Coast from an urban area in western Mexico all the way to northern Alaska. A branch of that road ran through the Sonoran Desert and up onto the Colorado Plateau.

From the Pueblo communities of the Southwest, travelers took roads eastward onto the semiarid plains along tributaries of the Pecos River. Other roads led from the northern Rio Grande to the southern plains of what is now western Oklahoma by way of the Canadian and Cimarron Rivers. The routes along those waterways led to others that followed rivers from the Southeast and connected with roads that turned southward toward the Valley of Mexico.

From Muscogee (Creek) towns in present-day Georgia and Alabama, travelers could take a road north through Cherokee lands and over the eastern mountains to where the Ohio and Scioto Rivers met. From there, they could eventually reach the West Coast on a route that followed the Ohio, Mississippi, and Missouri Rivers, crossed the Rocky Mountains, and met the Columbia River road. Going even farther, they could reach the large population center at the river's mouth and connect with the Pacific Coast road.

When Europeans arrived on this continent, they often seemed unaware that many conditions that were useful to them were the result of Indigenous peoples' stewardship of the land. Some early settlers remarked that in many places they could easily have driven carriages between the trees. Others commented about large clearings in the forests, some with well-tended gardens and cornfields. They did not seem to recognize that for thousands of years Native people had been making roads and clearing spaces to make trading, hunting, and agriculture easier. Willfully or not, they depicted the land as empty, devoid of "civilized" peoples—and theirs for the taking.

North America in 1492 was not a virgin wilderness. It was a network of Indigenous nations, a network of peoples of the corn. The link between peoples of the North and the South can be seen in the diffusion of corn from Mesoamerica along routes created by the people and used for millennia.

Both Muscogees (Creeks) and Cherokees, for example, whose original homelands in North America are located in the Southeast, trace their lineage to migration from or through Mexico. Cherokee historian Emmet Starr (who uses the spelling "Muskogee") wrote:

> The Cherokees most probably preceded by several hundred years the Muskogees in their exodus from Mexico and swung in a wider circle, crossing the Mississippi River many miles north of the mouth of the Missouri River as indicated by the mounds. . . . The Muskogees were probably driven out of Mexico by the Aztecs, Toltecs or some other of the northwestern tribal invasions of the ninth or preceding centuries. This is evidenced by the customs and devices that were long retained by the Creeks.[2]

Seeds were stored in seed pots from one season to the next. The small opening kept the corn safe from rodents. The design on this modern seed pot by Pearl Talachy of Nambé Pueblo depicts a corn plant.

Traditions related to corn are practiced throughout the Indigenous agricultural areas of North America. Some elements are similar to those in the Valley of Mexico. Although these practices vary from one community to the next, at the core of each dance, of each song, of each prayer is a commemoration of the gift of corn. The peoples of the corn remain connected in spite of the heavy influences of colonialism.

■ ■ ■

This brief overview of precolonial North America counteracts the settler-colonial myth of the wandering

Neolithic hunter and vast unused and uncharted lands. Indigenous civilizations were based on advanced agriculture and well-developed systems of governance. It is essential to understand the complex interrelationships Indigenous peoples had before European invasions.

It is also essential to understand that those relationships have evolved in ways that continue to bring Indigenous people from around the world to protect key resources from exploitation. In 2016 and 2017, Indigenous people from six continents came together to resist construction of a pipeline that endangered water resources. They took a stand as stewards of the land, supporting each other's struggles into the twenty-first century. They stood together at Standing Rock.

Native people today are still involved in protecting their communities and their resources. This photograph shows members of many tribes who gathered at Standing Rock in North Dakota in an effort to stop a pipeline that threatened an essential water source.

CHAPTER TWO

CULTURE OF CONQUEST

If you want to fully understand what Europeans did when they encountered the Indigenous peoples of the Americas, it helps to know what happened in Europe in the centuries before 1492. Several closely related developments in Europe affected how Europeans viewed the land and the Indigenous peoples. Those developments include religious warfare, the notion that land should be private property, the concept of white supremacy, and the desire for gold. A later development was the idea of terminal narratives, which were theories put forth to explain colonization of the Americas.

■ HOW IT BEGAN

Europeans who colonized the Americas came from their own rich, ancient cultures. Their many societies had developed rigid social and economic class structures in which wealth and power were concentrated among monarchies, aristocracies, and the Catholic Church. These influential institutions and individuals were driven by greed and lust for power to exploit and attack others outside Europe.

The inhabitants of Europe practiced a variety of religions prior to encountering Christianity. Research shows that these religions differed from Christianity in many

Other can imply "not like me" or "not like us." Many societies, or groups in a society, identify as Us or We and view people outside their group as They or Them. This is a typical human response to recognizing differences that can become a problem when more than one group wants or needs the same resources. Then, the groups may begin to emphasize the differences and frame them as a threat.

Treating differences as a threat enables one society to dehumanize the other. It allows them to rationalize using violence against the other and destroying their culture. It can create what some anthropologists call a culture of conquest. Sometimes a culture of conquest moves against people within its own society, and sometimes it moves against other nations or groups on other continents. Can you think of time when you have heard people speak of a group or person in ways that dehumanize them, ways that make them a threatening Other?

ways, including the power that women could hold in rituals. The Christian religion gained influence in Europe over several centuries, gradually overcoming the old religions practiced by the people living there. Conversion from the old religions to Christianity took several forms across Europe: sometimes through peaceful persuasion, sometimes through conquest.

By the eleventh century CE, Christianity in the form of Catholicism was the dominant religion in Europe, and church leaders held a great deal of political power. Beginning with Pope Urban II, the church leadership and the European monarchies sought to bring Christianity as far East as possible and to take over Muslim-controlled trade routes in the process. These campaigns were called the Crusades and were framed as religious wars between Christianity and Islam. But history strongly suggests that the ultimate goal for the church and the European rulers was about more than winning souls to Christianity. It was about gaining wealth and power through conquest.

Most of the soldiers in the Crusades were recruited from the peasantry. Peasants were people who were forced into poverty when the aristocracy took over all the land they had once used. If they served as soldiers, they had the right to sack and loot Muslim towns and cities, which would gain them wealth and prestige back home.

Toward the end of the thirteenth century, the Catholic Church began what could be called a series of domestic crusades within Europe. The church directed soldiers to crush "enemies" in their midst—people who questioned or did not follow church doctrine, women who were suspected of witchcraft, and commoners in general. This allowed knights and nobles to seize land and force the commoners who lived on it to work for them. These domestic crusades terrorized poor people and, at the same time, got them involved in what was painted as a holy adventure: turning all Europe into a Christian land. Many Christian commoners were tricked into believing that their religion and their cause made them superior to those they fought against as soldiers.

◼ LAND AS PRIVATE PROPERTY

For centuries, people in Britain and the rest of Europe grew crops and grazed livestock on large areas of land that were not owned by anyone. These areas were called the commons. Any person in the community could use the land. They could raise livestock and crops, using what they needed and selling the surplus.

During the Crusades era, European nobles took over the commons so they could own it. Land went from being accessible to all to

When the nobles appropriated the commons, they created a peasant class that had little choice but to work for the landowners. This painting shows peasants toiling in a field while an overseer wields a staff.

being private property where no one could go without permission from the owners. This completely changed the structure of communities and created a peasant class, who were forced to work for the landed class and to fight in their wars. Later in Britain, laws were changed to "enclose" the commons and keep people from hunting game or raising their crops and livestock there.

Wool was central to the British economy and was especially important during the sixteenth and seventeenth centuries CE. On the land taken from the commons, landowners were able to employ laborers from the peasant class to raise large herds of sheep and to send the wool to factories to be processed. These woolen factories became major employers of people whose families had been displaced when land was privatized. Adults and children alike worked on the farms and in the factories. They made little money and the working conditions were poor, even dangerous.

Although many commoners converted to Christianity, they held on to many aspects of their pre-Christian life.

This included the esteem accorded to women who held life-giving roles as healers and midwives. To undermine the status of these women, some people with influence began depicting women's power as backward or evil. This sometimes took the form of accusing women of practicing witchcraft. If a child died mysteriously, someone in the community could single out a woman and accuse her of using witchcraft to kill the child. Those accused of being witches were usually poor peasant women, often widows. Their accusers tended to be wealthier individuals who controlled local institutions or had ties to the national government, and were sometimes even the women's landlords or employers.

Some of these traumatized common people, and their descendants became the settlers who would cross a vast ocean, drawn by the promise of their own land and higher status. They brought the practice of witch hunting with them to what became Virginia and Massachusetts. There, they quickly called Indigenous populations "children of Satan" and "servants of the devil." In this way they could justify treating the Indigenous peoples in much the same ways they had been treated when the nobles displaced them from the commons.

WHITE SUPREMACY AND CLASS IN EUROPE AND THE AMERICAS

By the time of the Crusades, the Catholic Church had become a political force that sought to dominate all Europe. Although the majority of the population had—by choice or by force—become Christian, the church saw Europe's Jews and Muslims as threats to its power. To address these perceived threats, an idea emerged that allowed the church to grant privileges to "Old Christians" and excluded anyone who converted from other religions. That idea is limpieza de sangre, meaning "cleanliness of blood." "Blood" and "bloodlines" were a way of talking about people's ancestry. Church leaders became focused on how far back a person's ancestors had been Christian, believing that the longer a person's Christian bloodline, the purer and cleaner it must be. The idea evolved into discriminatory laws by which individuals and whole groups of people could be judged to be unclean or impure. Even Jews and Muslims who had converted and their descendants were considered to be impure.

Christians who could prove blood purity might live in dire poverty but could claim a certain amount of equal status with aristocrats. Even though they had no money or land, they could say their blood was as pure as that of a noble, and that pure blood made them superior to anyone who was not Christian and to new converts to Christianity. The notion of blood purity led to brutal persecution of Jews, Muslims, and many others during the Inquisition and the Crusades.

This idea that "bloodline" is more important than wealth or social status laid the groundwork for what we call, today, white supremacy—the mistaken and self-serving belief that light-skinned or white people are superior to those with darker skin and therefore should be the dominant group in society. Because of the influence of the church in Europe, Christianity came to be identified with being European, being light-skinned. As those light-skinned Christian Europeans became interested in conquering other places, they took with them the assumptions that they were inherently superior to many of the peoples they encountered. Their belief in white supremacy made it possible for them to think it was acceptable to enslave or eradicate those other peoples. Throughout recorded history, the targets of white supremacy have generally been Jews, Muslims, and people of other religions and people with dark skin (whether or not they were Christian). The enslavement of Africans for labor in the Americas is one example. Another is the Holocaust, when German Nazis and their allies murdered millions of European Jews along with people of other religious and ethnic minorities, LGBTQ people, and people with disabilities. White supremacy was also a significant factor in what happened to Native peoples in what came to be called the United States of America.

CONSIDER THIS

Let's look at the purity of blood idea. The notion of blood purity based on a family's history of being Christian traveled to what came to be called the Americas. It was quickly translated into a hierarchy based on "bloodlines" (which were expressed in color of the skin). The casta (caste) painting from seventeenth-century Mexico shown on the facing page depicts sixteen possible combinations of bloodlines, with a name for each category.

The idea of bloodlines has given way today to looking at DNA to identify ancestry. People send DNA samples to testing companies that promise to help them learn more about their ancestors. Some companies tell customers that their test results indicate they have Native ancestry. For some, that information is a surprise. For others, it confirms a family story. But an analysis of DNA cannot tell anyone they are part of a specific nation, and simply having Native ancestry does not give them authority to speak as a Native person. People who think they are Native American but but have not grown up in a Native community may lack tribally specific knowledge and are vulnerable to stereotypes and other misconceptions about being Native. One of the DNA testing companies, Viaguard, advertised that it could help people become enrolled in the Confederation of Aboriginal People of Canada. That group, however, is not recognized by either the National Assembly of First Nations or the Canadian government.

In 2018, the Canadian Broadcast Company (CBC) reported about a First Nations man who wondered about the legitimacy of Viaguard's testing. He sent three DNA samples, labeling them as his own, his father's, and his son's. Two were his own, but one was of a dog's saliva. All three test results were identical, saying that they had 12 percent Abenaki and 8 percent Mohawk ancestry— even the dog! The potential for fraud is significant. If you or someone you know plans to do a DNA test, make sure you do careful research before selecting a company, and be aware that most tribal nations do not accept DNA test results to determine citizenship.

During the early seventeenth century the English conquered Ireland and declared a half-million acres of Irish land open to settlement. The settlers came mostly from western Scotland. England had already conquered Wales and Scotland, but before its assault on Ireland it had never attempted to replace such a large Indigenous population with settlers.

To accomplish this, the English started by attacking the ancient Irish social system. They forbade traditional songs and music, exterminated entire clans, and brutalized survivors. In the sixteenth century, Sir Humphrey Gilbert (the official in charge of the Irish province of Munster) ordered that

> the heddes of all those (of what sort soever thei were) which were killed in the daie, should be cutte off from their bodies and brought to the place where he [Gilbert] incamped at night, and should there bee laied on the ground by eche side of the waie ledying into his owne tente so that none could come into his tente for any cause but commonly he muste passe through a lane of heddes which he used *ad terrorem*. . . . [It brought] greate terrour to the people when thei sawe the heddes of their dedde fathers, brothers, children, kinsfolke, and friends.[1]

The same Sir Humphrey Gilbert who brutalized the Irish during the colonization of Ulster was placed in charge of the first English colonial settlement in North America in Newfoundland in the summer of 1583.

In both the Christian Crusades against Muslims and England's invasion of Ireland, "religious" warfare easily became genocidal. The key step was for one side to cast the other as less than human, as unworthy of respect or decent treatment. In both wars, one side painted the other as spiritually or biologically inferior. Some nineteenth-century English scientists misused Darwin's ideas to peddle the notion that the Irish and people of color descended from apes. The English, they argued, were descendants of man, who was created by God in God's own image. The English, then, were human beings. Others were not. Thus, political and religious ideas merged into a white supremacist way of viewing the world and its peoples.

GOLD FEVER

There are many examples throughout history of people acquiring power and wealth through conquest. Earlier in this chapter, we discussed the way in which the aristocratic classes of Britain and the rest of Europe created a permanent class of impoverished people by taking over the commons—land that had once belonged to communities to be used for crops and livestock. The majority of Britons and other Europeans then depended on a few wealthy people for employment and survival. This was just part of the effort made by the landed classes at the time to take control of all available resources, which created conditions of servitude for those who no longer possessed any resources except for their bodies, their labor, and their ability to work.

Some resources, like wool, had real value. Woven into clothing, it provided warmth. It could be used in trade for other items. The value of some resources, however, is assigned by the most powerful people in a society. Gold, for example, is too soft to be made into tools for farming or building. Its value was created by those in power. They used it as decoration to show their wealth and they used it as currency. They wanted more and more of it.

Gold fever drove monarchs and others with wealth to fund colonizing ventures to find the metal. Perhaps the most famous example of such ventures would be the voyages of Columbus, which were supported by King Ferdinand and Queen Isabella of Spain.

DID YOU KNOW?

People used iron to make objects such as these Crusades-era forks (left), because it is strong enough for tools and other items needed for daily life and for farming, hunting, and warfare.

Gold is too soft for practical uses. It can be molded with bare hands, but unlike silver and some other metals, it does not dissolve in certain acids. Its beauty and ability to be easily shaped make it ideal for jewelry. Its rarity made it expensive, and thus the European royalty and nobility considered it the perfect material for their adornments, such as this crown, containing the Polish crown jewels (right).

On his first voyage in 1492, Columbus started a colony of about forty men on the island he called Hispaniola, which is currently divided into the nations of Haiti and the Dominican Republic. He returned to Spain with gold and a number of Arawak people he had enslaved. The next year he returned to the island with seventeen ships and a thousand men. He found that Arawaks had fought and killed the men he had left there to colonize their island. He started another settlement and went back to Spain, this time kidnapping four hundred Arawak people to serve as slaves.

In 1494, knowing what Columbus had found, the monarchs of Spain and Portugal along with the pope of the Catholic Church made a treaty that divided what they called the "New World" between the two nations. They drew a line from Greenland south through what is now Brazil. They claimed that possession of the entire world west of that line would be open to Spanish conquest. Everything east of it was for Portuguese conquest.

Driven by the desire for gold, Columbus would make two more trips. Others, like Vasco Núñez de Balboa, Juan Ponce de León, Hernando Cortés, and Ferdinand Magellan made similar journeys. Their names and voyages are well known. They are all celebrated as "courageous explorers" or "brave conquistadores," but their primary motivation was greed. In some places where they waged war on Indigenous peoples, they destroyed magnificent statuary and artworks just to take the gold and silver the artisans used.

Explorer and conquistador alike were ultimately seeking gold for themselves and their sponsors. The destruction of humanity they wrought in that quest was not, and is not, seen for what it was: absolute greed and cruelty.

Historians have two primary theories to explain what allowed the Europeans to thoroughly colonize the Indigenous lands in North America. One is that Indigenous peoples were overwhelmed by superior military campaigns. Another is that the Indigenous populations were decimated by diseases brought by the Europeans such as smallpox and diphtheria. These theories are sometimes called "terminal narratives." The word *terminal* suggests that Native nations and the peoples in them were completely wiped out by Europeans. That is not the case. Military campaigns and disease did have a devastating impact on Indigenous peoples, but efforts to exterminate them were not successful.

Neither of these terminal narratives explains why conflict between the colonizers and the Indigenous peoples continued for three hundred years before the United States was formed. They do not explain why the US military waged a ground war against Indigenous nations for more than a century after that, and why conflict continues today in the courts of the United States.

In the Americas, European colonizers used strategies they had used in Ireland, Africa, and Asia. The different European governments frequently pitted one Indigenous nation against another. Another especially effective strategy was disruption of the Indigenous trade networks, which caused food shortages and starvation. This forced some Native communities to depend on the colonizers for supplies. And of course, outright violence against Indigenous peoples by European forces occurred frequently.

In spite of everything in the European arsenal of conquest, Indigenous peoples survived more than five centuries of campaigns to take over their land and resources. Today, the presence of more than five hundred federally recognized nations is evidence of the successes Native peoples had as they fought to protect their nations, their homelands, and their families.

TO DO

There were 573 sovereign tribal nations as of December 15, 2018, each with the recognized power to govern and exist as an independent entity. How many can you name in three minutes? Let's see! Set a timer on a cell phone, watch, or oven; punch in three minutes; and see what you can do. Then, do an internet search for "Indian Entities Recognized and Eligible to Receive Services from the United States Bureau of Indian Affairs." Each year, the federal government publishes a list of those Native entities in its federal register. Are the ones you listed there?

* * *

Most of the Europeans who traveled to what they called the New World in 1492 and after were those whose families had been displaced when the commons were converted to private property. They carried with them a hunger to own land and other forms of wealth, including gold. They believed that by virtue of being white and Christian, they were superior to the Indigenous peoples they encountered.

Over the following centuries, their descendants would develop those terminal narratives—stories about the end of Indigenous peoples—to explain and justify their actions. Those Indigenous peoples and their descendants resisted invasion of their homelands and centuries of destruction and exploitation by the colonizers. Today they speak back, as individuals and as sovereign nations, against ongoing trauma and the consequences of conquest and terminal narratives. With their bodies, their art, and their words, they tell a different story.

CHAPTER THREE

CULT OF
THE COVENANT

This chapter looks at the religious and philosophical foundations of the permanent English colonies in North America. The first two such colonies were founded by separate but similar religious groups, the Pilgrims and the Puritans. They believed that as part of their covenant with their god, they should create "godly" societies in the "New World." Their commitment to their religious teachings was so focused that it is not unreasonable to describe them as cults.

DEFINITION

In a religious context, *cult* refers to a relatively small group of people dedicated to a set of beliefs that are outside mainstream theology. For example, the Pilgrims who colonized Cape Cod could be considered a Protestant Christian cult because their beliefs were in opposition to Catholicism and other dominant Protestant religious thinking of the time. Cult members, who tend to be firm believers in their system, generally do not consider themselves to be in a cult.

MYTH OF THE PRISTINE WILDERNESS

What do you imagine North America looked like when colonizers first came from Europe? Do you picture it as an untouched, green wilderness with a small scattered population of primitive people, or with no people at all? Your mental image has probably been influenced by paintings and movies about that time. That mental image most likely includes depictions of Pilgrims or Puritans in a prayerful pose. Their Christian Bible has a line in it that seemed to shape how they went into that wilderness: "For all the land which thou seest, to thee will I give it, and to thy seed for ever." (Genesis 13:15, King James Version)

Those images do not reflect the presence of roads, cities, towns, villages, and trading networks you read about in chapter 2. Native peoples had created town sites, farms, monumental earthworks, and networks of roads, and they had devised a wide variety of governments, some as complex as any in the modern world. They had developed sophisticated philosophies of government, traditions of diplomacy, and policies of international relations. They conducted trade along roads that crisscrossed the land masses and waterways of the American continents. Before the arrival of Europeans, North America was indeed a "continent of villages,"[1] as some historians have called it, but it was also a continent of nations and alliances among nations.

But the Doctrine of Discovery, which was ingrained in the mind-set of European colonizers, assured Christians that whatever land they saw was theirs to occupy and use. Their god, they believed, had given them dominion over the land and all its resources. In their eyes the land was an unoccupied, pristine wilderness. This idea is the basis of the origin story of the United States, a story that, like a myth, has been retold for hundreds of years.

If North America had actually been an undeveloped wilderness, the European settlers could not have survived. They lacked the financial means, the technology, and the social organization to maintain colonies so far from Europe. The colonizers' survival depended both on what they could learn from Indigenous peoples and on what they could take from them. They learned to grow plants Indigenous peoples had domesticated, such as corn, squash, and tobacco. They relied on local Indigenous people to help them find necessities such as water and medicinal herbs. The colonizers also stole farmland that was already cultivated. They took control of the deer parks that had been cleared and maintained by Indigenous communities. They traveled on overland and water routes the Indigenous peoples made, and ultimately, they used those routes to move their armies in wars against Indigenous nations and other European nations.

The European colonizers lacked the skills they needed to survive in this "pristine wilderness," but they had the skills, the technology, and the motivation for conquering other people, which is what they set about to do. As historian Francis Jennings writes,

> They did not settle a virgin land. They invaded and displaced a resident population.
>   This is so simple a fact that it seems self-evident.[2]

This invasion and displacement were not random occurrences. Some significant ideas about religion and culture provided justification and incentive for what happened.

THE CALVINIST ORIGIN STORY

The Europeans who came ashore at Cape Cod in November of 1620 carried a view of the world that was based on the teachings of Christian religious reformer John Calvin. Calvin objected to Europe's dominant religious doctrines of his time.

According to Calvin,

- Humans do not have free will and do not determine the course of their own lives. Everything that happens is the will of God.
- People's salvation is predestined, already decided by God, and has nothing to do with their actions while on earth.
- Certain individuals are "called" by God and are among the "elect."
- One is born as part of the elect or not, according to God's will.
- Outward good fortune, especially material wealth, is a sign of God's favor.

- Obeying lawful authority, even when one disagrees with it, is a sign of being one of the elect.
- Bad luck, poverty, and a rebellious attitude are all evidence of damnation.

As Calvinists, the Pilgrims and the Puritans thought, although they could never be certain, that they were among the elected few their god had chosen for salvation. They believed that they were called by their god to create a new place where they could practice their own religion without having to live among those who did not believe as they did. Both groups viewed the "New World" as a place where they could do that.

When the *Mayflower* landed at Cape Cod in 1620, forty-one of the men on board wrote an agreement for how their colony would operate. This Mayflower Compact invoked their god's name and declared that they and their fellow passengers on the *Mayflower* were

- loyal subjects of the king of England
- the "First Colony" in North America
- in a covenant that would be governed by "just and equal laws" that they promised to obey

Ten years later in 1630, Massachusetts Bay Colony was founded by the Puritans. This colony had two purposes. One goal was to establish trade in goods produced in the colonies. But it was also meant to be a godly community, a religious home for the Puritans, who did not tolerate dissenting views on spiritual matters. The Puritans saw the Indigenous people as incapable of salvation but still in need of aid, as the colony's official seal suggests. It depicts

Seal of the Massachusetts Bay Colony, around 1672.

a near-naked Native man holding a flimsy bow and arrow, and the plea "Come over and help us."

From the Pilgrims to the founders of the United States and continuing to the present day, the idea of a covenant involving people and God has persisted. In fact, it is the bedrock of US patriotism. The Declaration of Independence, writings of the "Founding Fathers," the US Constitution and

CONSIDER THIS

Notice that the man on the official seal of the Massachusetts Bay Colony is shown wearing only a bunch of leaves. From their first contact with Indigenous peoples to the present, non-Indigenous image makers have created images of Indigenous people that show them with very little clothing. At times, these depictions defy logic: showing people nearly naked in the dead of winter, as if they didn't know better, were impervious to cold, or were more animallike than human. In contrast, Europeans in North America are generally shown as being fully clothed, even in the sweltering heat of summer.

If you examine a selection of the countless images available of Native people and their material culture, you would see that most focus on clothing, tools, weapons, and homes. These are visible aspects of any culture, but there are not-visible aspects that are more important. Indigenous peoples of what came to be called the Americas were citizens of self-governing nations. What are some ways the images like the one on the seal, made by non-Indigenous people, might affect your ability to see, know, and understand Indigenous peoples?

its First and Second Amendments, Lincoln's Gettysburg Address, and the Pledge of Allegiance are all bundled into the covenant first expressed in the Mayflower Compact in 1620. The signers of the Mayflower Compact agreed that they would, "in the presence of God and one another, covenant and combine" themselves together in order to begin their lives in a land that was new to them. The men who signed the Declaration of Independence in 1776 proclaimed that they would, "with a firm reliance on the protection of divine Providence," "pledge to each other our Lives, our Fortunes and our sacred Honor." And then "four score and seven years" later, during a civil war, President Abraham Lincoln used the Gettysburg Address to inspire commitment to the covenant that had created the United States: "This nation, under God, shall have a new birth of freedom—and that government of the people, by the people, for the people, shall not perish from the earth." The US Constitution does not mention God or a covenant specifically, but by referring to "We, the people of the United States" and "a more perfect union," it implies that the decision to unite the separate states is an agreement among high-minded people to work toward a goal of monumental importance—much like the covenant the Pilgrims believed they were making with their god.

In the origin myth of the United States, these documents have sacred status. People tend to speak of them with reverence, and students may even be required to memorize and recite key passages.

Referring to them as sacred might feel uncomfortable, because the First Amendment of the Constitution tells us that this nation legally mandates separation of church and state. However, the existence of so many key documents that refer to the Christian god tells us the separation is not as clear as we might think it is.

Woven into the national identity of the US is the idea that the nation was created to be unlike any other nation on earth. Some historians and legal scholars refer to the United States as "a nation of laws." This means that, unlike the European monarchies that colonized the Americas, the United States is not supposed to be governed by a particular class or interest group, and the phrase implies that its actions should be considered beyond reproach. Many politicians and citizens speak with pride of "American exceptionalism." In their eyes, the nation's history and mission make it unique and superior to other nations, past and present, around the world. In fact, exceptionalist ideology has been used from the very beginning to justify appropriation of the continent and then domination of the rest of the world. It persists today, as is evident when the United States invades countries claiming to be rescuing them.

This "nation of laws" is also often called a "nation of immigrants." From its beginning, the United States and its citizens have welcomed, solicited, bribed, and forced people from other places to come to lands it said were "cleansed" of their Indigenous inhabitants. The country developed ways by which some could become formal citizens of this nation of laws. This citizenship process includes taking the Naturalization Oath of Allegiance to the United States of America, which says, in part:

> I will support and defend the Constitution and laws
> of the United States of America against all enemies,
> foreign and domestic; that I will bear true faith and al-
> legiance to the same; that I will bear arms on behalf of
> the United States when required by the law; that I will
> perform noncombatant service in the Armed Forces of
> the United States when required by the law; that I will
> perform work of national importance under civilian
> direction when required by the law; and that I take
> this obligation freely, without any mental reservation
> or purpose of evasion; so help me God.[3]

Immigrants who take the oath are pledging loyalty to the covenant. In theory, these naturalized citizens are equal in standing to those born in the United States. It is reasonable for them to believe they are exceptional too, and that they can depend on the laws to protect them. The historical record, however, tells us otherwise. At one time or another, the patriotism of particular immigrant groups—such as Italians, Germans, and the Japanese—has been questioned. Even those who were naturalized citizens were judged to be insufficiently loyal. Those who passed judgment on them have primarily been the descendants of Calvinist colonizers who spilled Indigenous blood, along with their own, fighting to take the land they believed their god said should be theirs.

As previously discussed in chapter 2, Britain's colonization of Indigenous lands in North America was foreshadowed by its colonization of the province of Ulster in northern Ireland. In the early 1600s, the British seized a half-million acres from Irish farmers, drove them from their lands, and opened those lands to settlers who would be under English protection. To invade and overwhelm the indigenous Irish in Ulster, the British Crown called upon recruits from Scotland, which Britain had already invaded and colonized.

Most of the Scots were Protestants who embraced Calvin's ideology. In Ulster, they created a Protestant presence within a predominantly Catholic nation and gave Britain a foothold for its efforts to expand its empire. In the early eighteenth century, large numbers of these Ulster Scots—or Scotch-Irish, as they called themselves—and their descendants pulled up stakes and crossed the Atlantic to the British colonies there. A number of them left Ireland for religious reasons, but most were victims of disastrous British policies that brought economic ruin to Ireland's wool and linen industries. A prolonged drought made matters worse. Many of these cash-poor Ulster Scots didn't have enough money to get to the colonies and chose to become indentured servants, which meant they agreed to work a set number of years for someone who would pay their passage.

The Ulster Scots became the core group of frontier settlers in North America. Before ever meeting Indigenous peoples in the Americas, they had already fought the indigenous Irish people for land, and they had perfected techniques of scalping their Irish victims for bounty.

CONSIDER THIS

Do you know the differences between indentured servitude and slavery?

Many people who didn't have enough money for passage to Virginia or another colony might choose to become indentured servants. This meant that they chose to enter contracts to work for no direct pay in exchange for passage across the Atlantic. In contrast, people who were enslaved were kidnapped and held against their will. They did not enter into agreements. They did not choose to go to the colonies.

As indentured servants, people agreed to work for employers for a set number of years, after which the agreement ended and the person was free to find other work. Some contracts also included a promise that they would be given some property or other goods when their term ended. By contrast, enslavement was intended to last a lifetime.

A person's indentured status did not pass to later generations, but children born to an enslaved person would also be enslaved.

Indentured servants had some legal protections. Indentured servants who ran away were considered to have broken a contract, but they were not considered property. People who were enslaved had no legal protections. They were considered to be property and could be bought or sold.

The record shows that people who were indentured servants were often treated harshly and could be severely punished for breaking the agreement. There is no evidence that enslaved people had good living conditions; in fact, the opposite was true, according to the historical record. A person who was enslaved was likely to be treated harshly and there was no end in sight for that treatment, other than escaping, which was extremely perilous.

As the Ulster Scots arrived in the British colonies, they settled in Pennsylvania and in other British-held areas on the homelands of several Indigenous nations.

The Ulster Scots were not merely settlers; they can be more accurately described as settler-soldiers. In wresting the lands from Indigenous peoples, they used the same violent tactics they had used against the Irish. Their modern descendants, however, tend to speak of their courage and valor. For example, Theodore Roosevelt once said that his Scotch-Irish forebears were "a stern, virile, bold and hardy people who formed the kernel of that American stock who were the pioneers of our people in the march westwards."[4]

As Indigenous peoples forcibly resisted the invasion, fighting over the land continued and increased. Many Ulster Scots went on to become soldiers and officers of the regular army. They also joined the frontier-ranging militias that cleared areas for settlement by exterminating Indigenous farmers and destroying their towns.

Some of these Ulster Scots became rich and powerful. Some had businesses, and some owned plantations that were worked by enslaved Africans. For many, however, warfare was a significant part of life in the decades leading up to the war for independence from Britain. For example, in the French and Indian War Ulster Scots fought with the British against the French and their "Indian" allies. Much of that war was actually fought in Europe by France and Britain, but it spilled into French and British colonies in North America, where much of the fighting was done by Indigenous allies of both sides.

By the time of US independence, significant numbers of Ulster Scots lived in the colonies, especially in the areas away from cities and towns. During the war for settler independence from Britain, the Ulster Scots were in the forefront of the struggle and formed the backbone of George Washington's fighting forces.

During the first two decades after the war for independence from Britain, large numbers of first- and second-generation Ulster Scots moved westward into the Ohio Valley, western Virginia, Kentucky, and Tennessee. In fact, they were the largest ethnic group in the westward migration. Many acquired and lost land several times before settling more permanently. Ulster Scots settlers were primarily farmers who cleared forests and built log cabins. But they also destroyed Indigenous farms, gardens, and towns, killing men, women, and children and taking over stores of food in addition to their lands. These God-fearing Calvinists formed a wall of colonization for the new United States.

The Ulster Scots had a key role in shaping not just the geography of the United States but also its political leadership. Beginning with Andrew Jackson in 1829, seventeen presidents of the United States have been of Ulster Scots lineage, including Ronald Reagan, the Bushes, Bill Clinton, and Barack Obama. In addition to serving as presidents, educators, and businessmen, the Ulster Scots instilled in mainstream US culture a strong set of Calvinism's individualist values. They continued to regard themselves as people of the covenant, selected and commanded by their god to go into the wilderness to build the new promised land. These settler-soldiers perfected an approach to warfare that formed the basis of US militarism into the twenty-first century. The Ulster Scots saw themselves, and their descendants see themselves, as true and authentic patriots, entitled by blood sacrifice to independence and Indigenous land. Indigenous peoples see the bloody footprints they left as they crossed the continent.

SACRED LAND BECOMES REAL ESTATE

To this day, for Indigenous peoples the land and its resources are "home" and exist for the common good of the people who share it. Particular places might hold spiritual or religious significance for any Indigenous nation, such as a place mentioned in an origin story or where ancestors are buried. Such areas are considered sacred, and the people treat them with reverence.

Europeans had no such connections to North American lands. To them, the land was a commodity to be acquired and sold for the benefit of individuals. It was mainly the wealthier Europeans who became land barons, plantation owners, and successful businessmen in the colonies. They would also become the key decision makers in the new republic. As owners of land, the Ulster Scots could think of themselves as wealthy, as having their own kingdoms to rule over. But in fact, they were not of the ruling class. The Ulster Scots were, for the most part, foot soldiers in the formation of the North American empire.

Their ability to own land made it seem that the new country was a more class-free and democratic society. For people of European ancestry, social class divisions were certainly more fluid in the United States than they had been in Europe, but the United States was never an entirely classless society. Indeed, class mattered a great deal. As the country grew, some descendants of the first Ulster Scots settlers were able to gain entry to the ruling class. When they did, they usually left behind their Calvinist denominations and became members of the elite church linked to the state Church of England.

■ ■ ■

With utter disregard for the Indigenous ways of thinking about the land, both sacred and nonsacred, the colonizers viewed all the land and resources they saw as things to own and to exploit. They believed that their god told them it was theirs for the taking, even if that meant blood would be spilled.

The idea of a society formed through a sacred covenant between God and people whom he has chosen lives on today in American exceptionalism: the notion that the United States of America was destined to be like no other place on earth; that it is carrying out a unique and essential mission "under God" and is therefore exempt from criticism.

CHAPTER FOUR

BLOODY FOOTPRINTS

As you know from previous chapters, Indigenous peoples had highly organized societies and systems of governance. When peaceful relations between their nations broke down and conflict arose, they also employed their own methods of warfare. These methods varied by nation, but historians note that, in general, Indigenous peoples fought to capture rather than kill their enemies. Conflicts came to an end with diplomatic negotiations. When the English began to invade their homelands, Indigenous peoples brought their ways of diplomacy to their interactions with the colonizers.

All the early English colonizers of North America, including those who came for religious reasons, had sworn loyalty to the king of England. The king had declared that large amounts of territory on the continent belonged to England. This meant, among other things, that the colonizers expected support from the Crown, including money for defense against Indigenous peoples who fought back against the invasion of their homelands.

To Indigenous peoples, these colonizers sometimes seemed—and often were—incompetent and virtually helpless. But it soon became clear that they felt entitled to take Indigenous land and resources for the king or for themselves. They were driven by greed and willing to do just about anything to acquire what they wanted.

This included acts of genocide.

◼ WAYS OF WAR AND THE ROOTS OF GENOCIDE

From the time the first European colonies were established, Indigenous nations found themselves in ongoing conflict with a people who seemed united in their desire to take over Indigenous homelands and eliminate Native peoples in the process. Throughout this chapter, we will examine some significant conflicts between specific Indigenous nations and European invaders of their homelands during the years from the early 1600s to the late 1700s. In all these conflicts, the colonizers—including those called Americans after settler independence from Britain—used regular and irregular warfare to secure their ultimate goal: removal of Indigenous peoples from the land to clear it for European settlement.

Generations of settlers, mostly farmers, gained experience as "Indian fighters," although they were not

CONSIDER THIS

Shortly after World War II, when the Holocaust was much on the minds of people around the world, the United Nations drafted an agreement that defined genocide in legal terms and listed crimes that can be punished under the agreement.

Generally speaking, writers avoid using the word *genocide* in history and textbooks about North America and the United States. Where have you seen the word used? What do you think might be the reason for not using it?

DEFINITION

According to military theory, "regular warfare," or "conventional warfare," refers to war between two or more nations, using battlefield tactics and typical weapons of war. The purpose of conventional warfare is to inflict damage on the opponent's military forces. Harm to civilians is not seen as part of regular warfare. In the modern world, it is often considered a violation of international law.

Irregular warfare is war in which one or more sides might not use a regular military organization, and might or might not use conventional weapons or tactics. Harm to civilians is an integral part of irregular warfare. Scalping, attacks on women and children or threatening to attack them, and the use of biological weapons such as smallpox were irregular warfare strategies employed against Indigenous civilian populations.

necessarily in the regular military. From the beginning, settlers organized units of irregular fighters to terrorize and destroy Indigenous communities by killing unarmed women, children, and elders. Then and now, being an "Indian killer" was often regarded as heroic. But in fact, murdering innocent people and burning their homes and fields requires very little courage or sacrifice.

In North America this kind of warfare was fueled by the desire to seek not just a military victory but also the complete annihilation of Indigenous peoples. Military historian John Grenier observes that any time it appeared that the Indigenous population might outnumber settlers in a region, the settlers were quick to resort to "extravagant violence."[1] As the settlers were outnumbered across most of the continent until the first decade of the nineteenth century, this meant that their interactions with Indigenous peoples were defined by violence for two hundred years.

Initially the British Crown did not provide much regular military support to the settlers in its colonies. Colonial leaders had to assemble their own armies. For example, military historian John W. Shy noted that when John Smith of the Jamestown colony wrote of his "soldiers," he meant only those men who at that moment had guns in their hands and who had been ordered to help him look out for danger.[2]

The more accurate term for Smith's armed force was *militia*. Most history textbooks about the colonial period refer to the militias, which were organized groups of armed farmers or townspeople, not trained professional soldiers. The first British colonial militias fought Indigenous people and French and Spanish colonizers. Later, during their war for independence from Britain, the separatists relied on militias to fight the British and their Indigenous allies. In many places militia members far outnumbered soldiers in the professional Continental Army led by George Washington.

DEFINITION

Separatists are people or groups who seek to become independent of the nation that has power over them and to form their own government.

The militias were not the only settler groups Indigenous peoples fought as they fended off invasion. Another was the rangers.

Rangers were men organized specifically to fight Indigenous peoples using tactics and strategies of wilderness warfare. They "ranged" (hence their name), usually in groups, between forts and settlements in and near

DID YOU KNOW?

You may not have heard of the rangers of the 1600s before, but you may know about the Texas Rangers baseball team. Over time, many sports teams adopted a name, logo, or mascot that could stir fans by encouraging them to think of sports games as warlike events. In this instance, the baseball team is using imagery associated with a fighting force organized in the 1800s to attack Indigenous people who were protecting their homelands from white settlers. The Texas Rangers are now a law enforcement agency, but their predecessors of the 1800s have long been romanticized (idealized and treated as unrealistically heroic)—for example, in Hollywood films and television shows such as *The Lone Ranger*. What other sports team names can you think of that refer to armed conflict? Which ones seem to be related to Indigenous peoples?

Indigenous territories. The first settler-organized ranger force was formed in 1676 in Plymouth, Massachusetts. Colonial governments, and later the United States, frequently deployed rangers to quash Indigenous resistance and displace Indigenous nations. Ranger groups were sometimes trained in especially violent irregular warfare by veterans of conflict in Europe.

The general goal of both the regular army and the irregular colonial forces was to destroy Indigenous communities. That usually meant targeting nonfighters such as Indigenous women, children, and elders with especially brutal acts. These included beheading, scalping, enslavement, and destroying entire villages and food supplies. Some military leaders even expressed interest in the use of biological warfare.

During the Pequot War (1636–1638), Connecticut and Massachusetts colonial officials began offering bounties for the heads of murdered Indigenous people. This practice of taking and displaying the heads of enemies was a part of European military tradition. Later the bounties were paid only for their scalps, which were easier to carry. Scalp hunters included rangers, but ordinary settlers could also take in scalps for a reward. By the mid-1670s, scalp hunting had become part of an organized system throughout the colonies.

The colonial government in time raised the bounty for adult male scalps, lowered it for adult females, and eliminated it for Indigenous children under age ten. However, the age and gender of victims were not easily distinguished by their scalps. Scalp hunters would sometimes take children and women captive to sell into slavery in the West Indies or elsewhere. Scalp hunting and enslaving captives were profitable and aided the colonizers' efforts to intimidate or eradicate the Indigenous population. The settlers gave a name to the mutilated and bloody corpses they left in the wake of scalp hunts: redskins.

Today we often think of biological and chemical warfare as modern inventions. However, there is evidence

DID YOU KNOW?

Historian John Grenier reports that it could be quite lucrative to be a scalp hunter. In 1670, settlers who worked as laborers made two shillings a day. Bringing in a scalp made them two hundred shillings.[3] That is the same as $2,973 in US currency today.

It is easy to see how the government's payments encouraged scalping, especially for those who were in need of income.

that leaders were aware of and interested in the use of disease to make conquest easier. Very early on, the colonizers recognized that smallpox could easily wipe out an Indigenous population, leaving land available for settlement. Sometimes such an epidemic was regarded as a blessing from God. But the military also recognized the potential for disease to make their work easier. For example, Major General Jeffery Amherst, who commanded the British army in the Seven Years War (1756–1763) is best known for his support of using germ warfare against Indigenous peoples. "Could it not be contrived," Amherst wrote to a subordinate officer, "to Send the Small Pox among those Disaffected Tribes of Indians? We must, on this occasion, Use Every Stratagem in our power to Reduce them."[4]

The colonizer armies, militias, and rangers knew that obtaining the land would be easier if, in addition to attacking Indigenous people, they destroyed Indigenous towns and food supplies. Often they used a strategy of setting fire to towns as they attacked, killing those who fled their homes and burning alive those who stayed inside. In many instances, the colonizer forces burned fields and stole or destroyed the foods and seeds the people had stored.

All these actions, in effect, made Indigenous people homeless in their own homelands.

THE POWHATAN CONFEDERACY

The Powhatan Confederacy was an alliance of more than thirty Algonquian-speaking tribes. Their homeland in the early 1600s stretched from what is now called Chesapeake Bay, inland along the Chickahominy, Rappahannock, and Potomac Rivers. They were among the first

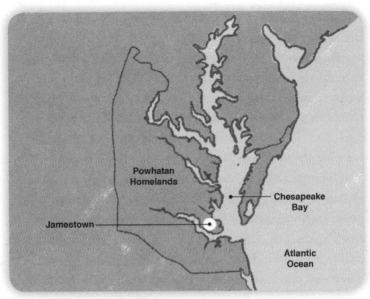

The Jamestown colony was built on Chesapeake Bay, at the edge of the Powhatan Confederacy homelands.

Indigenous peoples on the Eastern Seaboard to experience what can accurately be called an invasion of European colonizers. The site where the British chose to build Jamestown in 1607 was located on Powhatan territory in what the British called the Colony of Virginia.

The first Jamestown colonizers were among the many early arrivals who could not have survived without the help of Indigenous peoples. The colonizers apparently were not successful at growing crops or hunting. When they went foraging in the woods, Powhatans often harassed them, and coexistence between the two groups was uneasy. Their survival depended on ongoing diplomatic conversations between Wahunsonacock, the leader of the Powhatan Confederacy, and John Smith, leader of the Jamestown colony. These discussions included negotiating trading of corn and other foods for copper and other items the colonizers had brought.

Diplomacy failed when the harvest was poor. Smith threatened to harm Powhatan communities, including women and children, if the Powhatans did not provide the colony with food. Fighting began in 1609. Later that year John Smith returned to England after an injury. In his absence the English governor ordered George Percy, a nobleman and Jamestown resident, to take over and destroy the Indigenous population. Percy was a mercenary who fought in the Dutch war for independence from Spain. On August 9, 1610, Percy's forces attacked and burned an Indigenous town, killing many people. They also cut down all the corn growing in the fields and kidnapped the family of an important leader. On the way back to their ship, the militia beheaded a man they had captured when Percy criticized them for not having killed him outright. When they reached the ship, Percy's men threw the kidnapped children overboard and shot them in the water. An officer and two soldiers later removed the children's mother from the ship and killed her.

DEFINITION

A *mercenary* is a soldier for hire, who is not loyal to any particular government, group, or ideology.

Despite these brutal acts, the Powhatans continued to resist encroachment. They were successful in protecting their grain stores and, for a time, kept the British from moving beyond the Jamestown fort. Conflict continued over the next decade, with Jamestown residents frequently targeting Indigenous civilians. Undeterred, the Powhatans continued to build a stronger confederacy and attempted to discourage new English settlements along the James River. From 1610 to 1621 the relationship between the Powhatans and the colonizers remained strained and sometimes violent. Then, in 1622, the Powhatan Confederacy attacked several new settlements and killed nearly three hundred fifty people—about a third of the settler population.

Unable to eliminate the Indigenous population through open warfare, the British eventually launched a campaign of systematic destruction of the Powhatan agricultural resources. This series of raids against Indigenous fields and villages is sometimes called the Tidewater War (1644–1646), although it was not really a war but a series of attacks with the goal of starving the people out of the area.

THE PEQUOT NATION

The Pequots' homelands were the northeastern woodlands along the coast. Like the nations of the Powhatan Confederacy, the Pequots and their diplomatic allies spoke closely related Algonquian languages. Just before the 1620 landing of the *Mayflower*, smallpox had spread from English trading ships to the Pequot fishing and farming communities. The Calvinists aboard the *Mayflower* believed that the epidemic was evidence of God's grace and goodness, because it had greatly reduced the population of the area the Plymouth Colony would occupy. Indigenous people who survived had little means to immediately resist the settlers' takeover of their lands and resources.

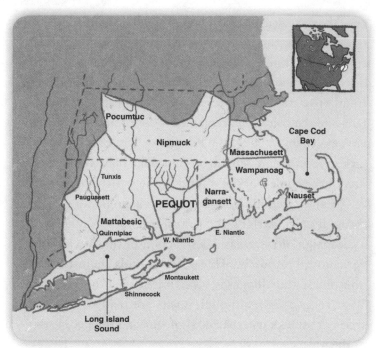

This map shows the homelands of the Pequot Nation, relative to neighboring nations in what are currently called the states of Connecticut, Massachusetts, and Rhode Island.

Sixteen years later, however, the Indigenous villages had recovered and were a barrier to the settlers moving into the Colony of Connecticut, which was in Pequot territory. A series of violent incidents triggered a brief but devastating war between the Pequots and the Puritans. The colony's records and many history texts refer to it as the Pequot War (1636–1638).

In 1636 the Pequots were blamed for killing an Englishman named Oldham. A force of soldiers under the command of John Endecott were sent to avenge his death. Endecott attacked some Indigenous towns, but there were few casualties. Many townspeople were hiding. He had his men burn the villages and food supplies. Shortly afterward, the Pequots, incensed by the assaults on their towns and their food supplies, attacked Fort Saybrook, at the mouth of the Connecticut River. The siege of the fort lasted until March 1637.

The colonial government retaliated by sending a force led by a mercenary named John Mason to Mystic River, where Pequots were living in two forts. In one fort were mainly Pequot men. In the other were primarily women, children, and elders. Mason targeted the latter. Slaughter ensued. After killing most of the Pequot defenders, the soldiers set fire to the structures and burned the remaining people there alive.

Though the Puritans' slaughter of the Pequots was devastating, they continued to fear retaliation by the surviving Pequots who had sought refuge among neighboring nations. The fear was so great that they destroyed the Pequot's remaining homes and food supplies and forced them to leave their homelands.[5]

THE CHEROKEE NATION

The homelands of the Cherokee Nation covered substantial parts of what is now Georgia, Tennessee, and the Carolinas. Their first contact with European settlers was with the Spanish, who began invading the southeastern Indigenous homelands in the mid-1500s. In the late 1600s, Cherokees likely first encountered the English when traders from the Virginia Colony came to the region.

Then in the 1680s rangers from the Carolinas began attacks on Native and Spanish settlements in Georgia. In the early 1700s South Carolina's governor led a raid

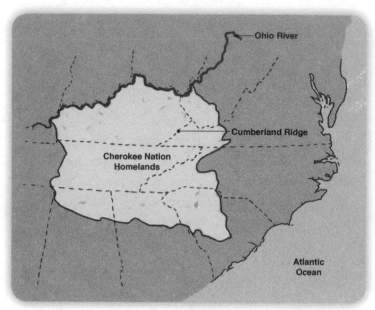

This map shows the boundaries of the original homelands of the Cherokee Nation, which included large parts of what are currently several states of the southeastern United States.

into the area and returned with more than four thousand Indigenous people whom he intended to sell into slavery.

From the time settlers first squatted on Indigenous land in the Southeast, rangers were in the forefront of genocide, clearing the region for British settlement as they had in New England. When the British established the colony of Georgia in 1732, its commander, General James Oglethorpe, commissioned a Scots Highlander, Hugh Mackay Jr., to organize and train his small regular army to become a Highland Ranger force.

The Highlanders were reputed to be tough, fearless fighters—in other words, brutal killers. The English rangers who had trained to fight like Highlanders were essential to Britain's invasion of Florida in 1739. In a conflict that lasted nearly a month, rangers and their Indigenous allies attacked Spanish and Indigenous towns and villages, looting and burning them, taking scalps, and hunting for people who had escaped slavery.

As tensions intensified between the Spanish in Florida and the southern British colonies, both the Spanish and the British sought to win over the Cherokee Nation as an ally. The Cherokees initially rejected Oglethorpe. Even when he did manage to win a commitment from some Cherokee villages in 1739, he knew that they might change their minds if they saw that siding with the British was not to their advantage.

During the 1740s the British War Office and Parliament commissioned two companies of colonial rangers and authorized more than a hundred men to serve in the Highland Rangers in Georgia. The importance of rangers to the defense and expansion of the colonies increased in the decades that followed.

In the French and Indian War (1754–1763), the British found that the Cherokee Nation was an extremely powerful ally to the French. In October 1759, the North Carolina governor presented the strategy that the British would use against the Cherokee:

> In Case a War must be proclaimed, the three Southern Provinces of Virginia and the Carolinas should exert their whole force, enter into and destroy all the [Cherokee] Towns of those at War with us, and make as many of them as we should take their Wives and Children Slaves, by sending them to the Islands [West Indies] if above 10 years old . . . and to allow 10 lbs sterling for every prisoner taken and delivered in each Province.[6]

In previous wars against Indigenous nations, British commanders had assigned ranger groups specific missions, but to fight the Cherokee, both the regular forces and the rangers would target even the elders, women, and children.

The British command was well aware that their military could not defeat the Cherokees in their own country even with irregular warfare. So they added three hundred rangers, forty local militia members, and fifty Native allies to their troop count. Their first target was a Cherokee town of about two hundred homes and two thousand people. British forces set all the homes and other buildings on fire. They picked off individuals who tried to flee. Others who hid inside were burned alive. One after another, towns were set ablaze until the Cherokees organized a resistance strong enough to lay siege to British forts. A year later British forces struck even harder, overwhelming the Cherokee and destroying their capital, Etchoe. The British then moved on, razing fifteen more towns and burning fourteen hundred acres of corn. At the end of this campaign, five thousand Cherokees were made refugees, and the number of deaths remained uncounted.

When the French and Indian War ended, the French left the region, ceding to the British all the land they had claimed east of the Mississippi River. As far as the British were concerned, this included Cherokee territory, although the Cherokee Nation had never agreed to be part of France. Despite the tremendous cost of the British attacks on its villages and crops, the enormous Cherokee Nation remained strong, with a well-functioning government.

Some years later when the colonies began fighting to separate from Britain, the Cherokee again found themselves in the middle of warring nations seeking to enlist them as allies. To win the Cherokees to their side, British authorities provided weaponry and money, while separatist representatives threatened the towns with complete destruction if they did not remain neutral. Neutrality was the most the separatists could hope for, given their history of attacking the Cherokee.

A few Cherokee towns that had been hit hardest by rangers responded by attacking squatter settlements, destroying several in 1776. Separatist leaders quickly announced their determination to destroy the Cherokee Nation. In the summer and fall of 1776, more than five thousand rangers from Virginia, Georgia, and North and South Carolina stormed through Cherokee territory. As Cherokees fled, abandoning their towns and fields, the attackers seized, killed, and scalped women and children, taking no prisoners.

By mid-1780 the Cherokee resistance regained momentum when they began raiding squatters' settlements within Cherokee territory. During the winter of 1780–1781, the seven-hundred-man Virginia militia wreaked destruction again in the Cherokee Nation. Historian John Grenier notes that the militia commander wrote on Christmas Day to Thomas

DID YOU KNOW?

Though most people associate Thomas Jefferson with the phrase "life, liberty, and the pursuit of happiness," his words and actions with respect to Cherokees show that he was selective in who was deserving of those "inalienable rights." On August 13, 1776, in a letter to Edmund Pendleton, a delegate to the First Continental Congress, he wrote that he hoped "the Cherokees will now be driven beyond the Mississippi."[7] Clearly, he did not consider the Cherokee to have those rights to life, liberty, and pursuit of happiness on their own homelands.

Jefferson, then a Virginia delegate to the Continental Congress, that a detachment had "surprised a party of Indians, [and taken] one scalp, and Seventeen Horses loaded with clothing and skins and House furnishings." The cargo the horses carried is a clear sign that these were not fighters but fleeing refugees. The commander also reported that his forces had thus far destroyed about ten of the principal Cherokee towns, along with several smaller villages.[8]

All told, more than a thousand Cherokee homes were laid waste during that winter and some fifty thousand bushels of corn and other provisions either burned or looted. At this point, the Virginia and North Carolina separatist authorities organized a force that swept through Cherokee towns, driving residents out into present-day middle Tennessee and northern Alabama, where the campaign of extermination continued. Even though many of their people were fleeing, the Cherokee Nation kept up their resistance. In 1782 the governor of North Carolina sent five hundred mounted rangers to retaliate, with orders to "chastise that nation and reduce them to obedience."[9]

It would take nearly a half century after US independence was won to accomplish what Jefferson had hoped for: the forcible removal of the Cherokee Nation to "beyond the Mississippi."

THE SHAWNEE AND DELAWARE NATIONS

When the colonies rebelled against British rule, the Shawnee and Delaware (or Lenape) were among the many nations that faced pressure to side with either the British or the separatists. Their homelands at the time covered a significant portion of the Northeast woodlands. The Shawnee lived primarily in what is now known as Pennsylvania and Ohio. Delaware homelands included parts of what are now New Jersey, New York, Delaware, and Pennsylvania.

In 1763 King George III of England declared that no British subjects should settle on Indigenous lands in the Ohio Country west of a "proclamation line."

This action angered both settlers who wanted to move into that region and the land speculators who sought to

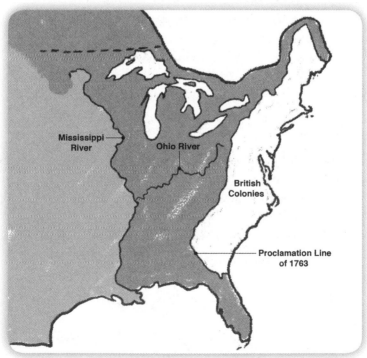

With the Proclamation of 1763, the British Crown established what it considered a clear boundary for its colonies along the Atlantic Coast.

profit from selling land there. One of those speculators was the British governor of Virginia John Murray, the Fourth Earl of Dunmore. He sided with British settlers who wanted land in the Ohio Country. In his view no royal policy could prevent settlers' seizure of Indigenous land.

Despite the Proclamation of 1763, squatters moved into the Ohio Country, settling on the farmlands and hunting grounds of the Shawnee Nation. In 1774 the Shawnee responded to these encroachments by raiding squatter settlements and expelling land surveyors. The settlers, and Dunmore himself, immediately retaliated. Dunmore commissioned 150 Virginia rangers to destroy Shawnee towns. He also mobilized the Virginia militia to invade the Ohio Valley, instructing them to destroy Shawnee towns and provisions and to "distress them in every other way that is possible."[11] During what became known as "Lord Dunmore's War," the Shawnees battled enemy forces that wanted to wipe them from the face of the earth.

As often happens in war, nations make difficult choices, and often there are disagreements on a course of action. Fearful that ongoing war would mean utter destruction of their nation, a faction of Shawnee accepted a peace agreement that meant giving up some of their autonomy and the territory they used as hunting grounds. Dunmore's War was only the beginning of a three-decade war between the settlers and the Shawnee Nation and its allies.

Their experience in Dunmore's War led the Shawnees to ally with the British against the separatists in 1777. They drove hundreds of squatters from settlements in

GEORGE WASHINGTON: HERO OR MONSTER? IT DEPENDS ON WHO YOU ASK!

In the early days of the US, some of the "Founding Fathers" worked as surveyors or speculators. Surveyors went across the land measuring and making maps for the colonial governments. While that seems like an interesting and innocent endeavor, the land they surveyed belonged to Indigenous peoples, who had not agreed to the Doctrine of Discovery. Surveyors measured and mapped the land in preparation for selling it out from under the Native people. George Washington was one of many surveyors whose work enabled them to increase their own landholdings. Washington was also a land speculator. That means he bought land that he had good reason to believe would soon become even more valuable—at which point he could sell it for a profit. Both surveyors and speculators served the goal of colonial growth, but their personal goals were likely to be self-serving: they could become wealthy with the knowledge contained in a map, while the colonies increased their land bases. Once land "belonged" to an individual or a speculator's land company, it could be protected by force against Indigenous peoples. Over and over, the work of the colonial surveyors and speculators led to destruction of Indigenous towns.

In fact, while many US history books depict George Washington as a heroic Founding Father and a surveyor too, Indigenous peoples do not think of him that way. The Seneca people gave him a name in their language to describe what he was doing: Conotocarious. It means "Town Destroyer." On December 1, 1790, Seneca chiefs sent a letter to George Washington. In it they wrote, "When your army entered the Country of the Six Nations, we called you the Town-destroyer and to this day, when that name is heard, our women look behind them and turn pale, and our children cling close to the neck of their mothers."[10]

their territory in the Upper Ohio Valley region. But when the tide of war turned against the British, the Continental Congress was able to focus on an offensive to annihilate the Shawnee Nation in the Ohio Country. They sent a force of five hundred fighters, both soldiers and irregular troops. Rampaging against innocent men, women, and children, they did not distinguish between different Native nations. Though their directive was to destroy the Shawnee Nation, they fell on the staunchly neutral towns of the Delaware Nation, torturing and killing women and children. In one particularly twisted incident, the settler troops slaughtered a Delaware boy who had been bird hunting alone. A near riot ensued over who had the right to claim the "honor" of the kill.

The newly formed US government began to move more aggressively to claim Indigenous lands and destroy Native nations. Its Continental Congress sent one thousand more soldiers and militiamen to the Ohio Country, where under the command of Brigadier General Lachlan McIntosh they were told to "chastise and terrify the savages, and check their ravages on the frontiers."[12] The Shawnee, having seen the separatists' brutal ways of war, moved their people to a place of relative safety.

The Delawares were on the receiving end of some of the worst violence against Indigenous peoples during the separatists' war against Britain. The Delaware Nation had determined that remaining neutral during the conflict would be their best chance of survival. Interactions with Moravian Protestant missionaries had shown the Delawares that Moravian ways of religion were similar to their own, including the ideal of pacifism. This led many Delawares to join the Moravian church and settle in what came to be known as Moravian Indian villages. One of these was named Gnadenhütten.

The decision to join the Moravian church made other Delawares uncomfortable. In 1781 the Delaware leader Buckongahelas addressed a group at Gnadenhütten, saying that he had known some good white men, but that the good ones were a small number and the rest could not be trusted:

> There is no faith to be placed in their words. They are not like the Indians, who are only enemies while at war, and are friends in peace. They will say to an Indian: "My friend, my brother." They will take him by the hand, and at the same moment destroy him. And so you will also be treated by them before long. Remember that this day I have warned you to beware of such friends as these. I know the long knives; they are not to be trusted.[13]

Buckongahelas's warning was prophetic. Within a year Gnadenhütten would be the scene of one of the most outrageous war crimes of that period.

As fighting continued, in 1781 in eastern Ohio, British troops displaced residents of the Moravian villages. They later allowed residents to return to Gnadenhütten to harvest their crops. In March of 1782 a settler militia from Pennsylvania, under the command of David Williamson, rounded them up, telling them they had to evacuate for their own safety. The militiamen confiscated anything that could be used as a weapon and announced that the Delawares were all to be killed. They were accused of giving refuge to some Delawares who had killed white settlers. They were also accused of stealing the household items and tools they possessed, because supposedly such items should belong only to white people. The condemned Delawares spent the night praying and singing hymns. In the morning, Williamson's men marched them in pairs into two houses and methodically slaughtered them—forty-two men, twenty women, and thirty-four children. One killer bragged that he personally had bludgeoned fourteen victims with a cooper's mallet, which he had then handed to an accomplice. "My arm fails me," he was said to have announced. "Go on with the work."[14]

The Gnadenhütten massacre was proof to Indigenous people that even being Christians and pacifists would not protect them.

THE HAUDENOSAUNEE CONFEDERACY

The Haudenosaunee Confederacy consisted of six distinct Iroquois nations—Mohawk, Seneca, Cayuga, Tuscarora, Onondaga, and Oneida—whose homelands included the western edge of the colony of New York. By the mid-1770s, as was the case everywhere else on Native homelands, settlers had already invaded and been squatting there. When the war between the British and separatists began, both sides vied to win the Haudenosaunee as allies.

As with the Cherokee Nation, both the British and the separatists sent representatives to the Haudenosaunee councils to appeal for their support. Each member nation had its own specific interests because each had had different experiences in the previous 150 years of British and French intrusion, including the French and Indian War. Pressure to take sides in the conflict caused fractures. In 1775 the Mohawk Nation allied with the British against the separatist settlers. The Seneca Nation had early on considered the British to be an intractable enemy, but with the separatist war looming they were more afraid of the settlers, and so the Senecas followed the Mohawks' lead into a British alliance. For the other nations in the confederacy, the benefits of allying with either side were not clear-cut. Initial allegiances shifted as the war went on, but in the end, all six of the Iroquois nations were seen as a threat to the separatists.

By 1779 General George Washington ordered preemptive action against the Haudenosaunee. He dictated to Alexander Hamilton a letter to be sent to Major General John Sullivan. His orders were

> to lay waste all the settlements around . . . that the country may not be merely overrun but destroyed. . . . You will not by any means, listen to any overture of peace before the total ruin of their settlements is effected. . . . Our future security will be in their inability to injure us . . . and in the terror with which the severity of the chastisement they receive will inspire them.[15]

Sullivan replied, "The Indians shall see that there is malice enough in our hearts to destroy everything that contributes to their support."

With the approval of the Continental Congress, three armies were mustered to launch an offensive against the Seneca and any other Indigenous nation that opposed the separatists. Their orders were to march across New York and into northern Pennsylvania, where they were to burn and loot all Indigenous villages and destroy their food supplies, turning the survivors into refugees. The separatist governments of the New York and Pennsylvania colonies offered rangers for the project. As an incentive for enlistment, the Pennsylvania assembly authorized a bounty on Seneca scalps without regard to sex or age. This combination of Continental Army regulars, rangers, and commercial scalp hunters ravaged most of Seneca territory. By 1781 Haudenosaunee towns and fields were in ruins.

■ ■ ■

The British colonizers were driven by the belief that they were entitled by divine decree and by royal declaration to live on and use the land and resources of North America. They saw Indigenous peoples as obstacles to what was rightfully theirs. They brought with them ways of warfare that meshed well with the goal of completely destroying an opponent, so that there was little need for diplomatic agreements that allowed the sides to coexist in the long term. They also adapted "new" tactics for wilderness warfare to support their overall goal of taking over the homelands of the Indigenous peoples.

As we look back, it is not hard to give a harsh name to what the settler colonials wanted and what they did: genocide.

From the first moment Europeans stepped onto what came to be known as North America, they left bloody footprints wherever they went seeking land and resources. They found, however, that Indigenous people were not easily scared off or conquered. Even after the birth of the United States, Native peoples would not get out of the way. They were determined to fight for their homelands, their communities, and their nations.

CHAPTER FIVE

THE BIRTH OF A NATION

The British withdrew from the fight to maintain their thirteen colonies in 1783. Negotiations to end the war gave birth to an independent nation: the United States of America. In the 1783 Treaty of Paris, the Crown ceded to the United States territory from the Mississippi River to the Atlantic Ocean, south of the Great Lakes and north of Spanish-occupied Florida. Much of that land, however, wasn't theirs to transfer. It still belonged to Indigenous nations, many of which had allied with the British in order to protect their homelands from land-hungry Americans. But no Indigenous nations were represented at the treaty negotiations in Paris; they were not invited or consulted.

▊ THE NEW ORDER

The end of the separatists' war for independence from Britain led to a new set of circumstances for Indigenous peoples. Some things remained the same—specifically, the determination of settlers and the new republic to force Indigenous peoples off their homelands to make way for settlement.

Among the new circumstances were the ways that treaties were written and viewed. Historians Vine Deloria Jr.

Although Indigenous peoples were not included in negotiating the Treaty of Paris, which ended the colonists' war with Britain, the treaty allowed the United States to claim millions of acres of Indigenous homelands—some of which are still contested.

and Raymond J. DeMallie note that traditionally when Indigenous nations entered into treaties, they considered *peace* to be more than an end to the fighting. Each side of the agreement had a moral duty to build and maintain a positive relationship with the others. On the other hand, Europeans viewed treaties as legal documents that focused on ending hostilities and as businesslike transactions where "the winner" got something from "the loser."[1]

Treaty making with Indigenous nations has a brief but important mention in Article 1, Section 8, of the Constitution. It says that Congress shall have the power to "regulate commerce with foreign nations, and among the several states, and with the Indian tribes."

For Indigenous peoples, this meant that they would be dealing with the centralized federal government rather than individual states about key matters such as trade and treaties. The Constitution's Second Amendment, the right to bear arms, does not mention Indigenous peoples, but it had a significant impact on them. It reads, "A well regulated Militia, being necessary to the security of a free State, the right of the people to keep and bear Arms, shall not be infringed." This meant that the irregular warfare waged by militias against Indigenous peoples in the colonial period would continue, approved by the central government and assured by the Second Amendment.

Between 1780 and 1815 the leaders of the new nation tried to go forward as "United" states but encountered resistance from settlers and from state governments. In particular, federal authority was questioned and tested west of the mountains from Canada to Spanish Florida. Many settlers on the borders of Indigenous territories believed that the newly created, professional US military might not support their interests. But in fact, the settlers' demands and actions led to federally sanctioned warfare against Indigenous peoples much as they had before the revolution.

Indigenous nations did not consent to a basic assumption of the Treaty of Paris: that they and their homelands were part of this "United States." As in the past, they met continued settler aggression with determined resistance. Their traditional diplomacy shaped new efforts to form alliances against the invaders. During the first three decades after the Treaty of Paris was signed, allied Indigenous nations in the Ohio Country and the southern states were involved in several struggles to resist settler encroachment.

INDIGENOUS ALLIANCES IN THE OHIO COUNTRY

Several Indigenous nations formed alliances in the heart of the Ohio Country. This included the Delawares, Miamis, Wyandots, and the Shawnees. The alliances were under the leadership of Meshekinnoqquah (Little Turtle), Weyapiersenwah (Blue Jacket), and Tecumseh.

In 1789 George Washington was sworn in as the first president of the United States. Because of the Treaty of Paris, Washington believed the US had sovereignty over the Ohio Country, a belief that was not shared by the people of the Indigenous nations who lived there. He had wanted to develop a professional army to enhance US prestige in the eyes of European countries. A professional army would also be less expensive than using mercenaries. But it became clear that at least in the short term, the army alone was no match for Indigenous resistance in the Ohio Country, and his first administration was thrown into a crisis by its inability to make Ohio available for settlers. On June 7, 1790, Secretary of War Henry Knox told an army commander that the frontier was so extensive that it would be "altogether impossible" to defend. The only solution he said, was to "extirpate, utterly, if possible" the Indigenous peoples who pushed back against settlements.[2] The army did not have enough professional soldiers to carry out Knox's orders. They would need mercenaries, so officers recruited men from militias made up of squatters from Kentucky. They were unaccustomed to army discipline but willing to exchange scalps for bounty or to kill Native people in exchange for a plot of land.

DEFINITION

To *extirpate* is to exterminate or destroy a living entity or group so completely that it ceases to exist forever.

This army moved to attack several Miami tribe villages but found them deserted. They set up a base in one village and waited for a Miami assault. But the assault never came. When the commander sent out small units to find the Miamis, their search-and-destroy missions were ambushed by allied Miamis and Shawnees under the leadership of Meshekinnoqquah and Weyapiersenwah. In response, Knox ordered the commanders to recruit five hundred Kentucky mounted rangers to burn and loot Miami towns and fields and to take hostages. They destroyed the Miamis' two largest towns and took forty-one women and children captive, then sent warnings to the other towns that the same would happen to them unless they surrendered unconditionally. Yet the allied tribes of the Ohio Country continued to fight despite the likely consequences.

In late 1791 the War Department put Major General "Mad" Anthony Wayne in charge of restructuring the army units under his command so they could function as irregular forces in Ohio. Between 1792 and 1794 Wayne put together a combined force of regulars and experienced rangers that would use tactics such as destroying food supplies and murdering civilians.

Wayne's units entered what is now northwestern Ohio and established a base they called Fort Defiance in the heart of an Indigenous alliance that included Delawares, Shawnees, Miamis, and Wyandots. Wayne issued an ultimatum to the alliance, threatening harm to women and children if the men did not stop fighting. When the alliance refused to submit, US forces destroyed Indigenous villages and fields and murdered women, children, and elders. They overpowered the alliance's main fighting force on August 20, 1794, at what is known today as Fallen Timbers, and for three days after the victory, laid waste to Indigenous houses and fields. The defeat at Fallen Timbers was a severe blow to the Indigenous nations of the Ohio Country, but they would reorganize their resistance during the following decade.

The Battle at Fallen Timbers and its aftermath were evidence that the federal government would not hesitate to use both regular and irregular warfare to get the lands it wanted. In the Treaty of Greenville, signed in 1795, the nations of the alliance ceded a great deal of their Ohio territory to the US. The treaty also stated that no citizen of the US, nor any white person, could settle on the remaining Indigenous land.

However, over the following decade more settlers poured over the Appalachians. They squatted on

Indigenous lands and built towns, confident that the US military would protect them. Faced with this ever-growing flood of squatters, two Shawnee brothers, Tecumseh and Tenskwatawa, began building a larger, more cohesive Indigenous resistance. The Shawnee community of Prophet's Town, founded in 1807 in what is now western Indiana, became their organizing center. From there, Tenskwatawa and others traveled throughout Shawnee country, calling on Shawnees to return to their traditional religions and cultural roots.

Tecumseh visited other nations, calling for unity in defiance of the squatter presence on their lands. He envisioned an alliance of all the peoples west to the Mississippi, north into the Great Lakes region, and south to the Gulf of Mexico. He hoped for an end of all sales of Indigenous lands to settlers to stop their spread into Indigenous lands. The alliance could then manage Indigenous lands as a federation.

The evolving Indigenous alliance posed a serious barrier to the United States' expansion. However, constant warfare was taking a toll on Indigenous peoples and their nations. In 1809 Indiana's territorial governor, William Henry Harrison, badgered and bribed a few destitute Delaware, Miami, and Potawatomi individuals to sign the Treaty of Fort Wayne. It stated that these nations would hand over their land in what is now southern Indiana in exchange for a yearly payment. Tecumseh promptly condemned the treaty and those who signed it without the approval of the peoples they represented.

Harrison met with Tecumseh at Vincennes in 1810. They came to no agreement, and met again in 1811. At that meeting Tecumseh had delegates with him from several nations, including Kickapoos, Wyandots, Peorias, Ojibwas, Potawatomis, Winnebagos, and Shawnees. After weeks of talks, nothing was resolved. Before leaving Vincennes, Tecumseh informed Harrison that he was traveling south to bring the Creeks, Choctaws, and Chickasaws into the alliance. Fearful of an even larger confederacy, Harrison reasoned that destroying Prophet's Town would crush the resistance. He decided to strike in Tecumseh's absence.

Harrison assembled Indiana and Kentucky rangers—seasoned Indian killers—and some US Army regulars. At the site of what is today Terre Haute, Indiana, the soldiers constructed Fort Harrison on Shawnee land. Tecumseh had told the people in Prophet's Town not to be drawn into a fight, because the alliance was not yet ready for war. But when US forces arrived on the edge of Prophet's Town on November 6, 1811, Tenskwatawa saw no alternative but to attack, despite his brother's instructions. He led an assault before dawn the following morning. Only after some two hundred of the Indigenous residents had fallen did the troops overpower the Shawnee. They burned and looted the town, destroyed the granary, and even dug up graves and mutilated corpses.

The destruction of Prophet's Town outraged Indigenous peoples all over the Ohio Country. Indigenous fighters went to a British garrison in Canada to obtain weapons and supplies, and Tecumseh called for a unified and coordinated Indigenous-led war on the United States. He invited Britain to join his forces if they chose, but it was to be an Indigenous-led resistance and his fighters would not take orders from British commanders. The United States was already on the verge of war with Great Britain, and this development was cause for more alarm. When President James Madison went before Congress seeking a formal declaration of war, he specifically referred to British support for Indigenous fighters on the frontier.

During the summer of 1812, the Indigenous alliance struck US forts and squatter settlements. They overwhelmed the forts at present-day Detroit and Dearborn and drove thousands of squatters from settlements all over Illinois and Indiana territories. The alliance seemed to have a reasonable chance of succeeding, but eighteen months of warfare severely depleted Indigenous villages and agricultural resources. Many Indigenous peoples were homeless and starving in their own homelands. When Tecumseh was killed in October 1813 at the Battle of the Thames, the alliance crumbled.

▓ MUSCOGEE AND CHEROKEE RESISTANCE

The Muscogee, or Creek, Confederacy included a number of Indigenous nations with homelands that covered much of present-day Georgia, Alabama, and parts of northern Florida. Their first European contact was with the Spanish; trade with the English began in the late 1600s.

The Muscogees officially remained neutral during the settler war for independence. However, in 1784, they turned to Spanish Florida for an alliance they hoped would stop the flow of squatters. Spain saw this arrangement as a buffer to its North American holdings, which at the time included the lower Mississippi and the city of New Orleans. The squatters considered the Muscogee Nation to be the main barrier to their permanent settlement in the region, particularly Georgia. The Muscogees called the squatters a name that, in their language, means "people greedily grasping after the land."[3]

INDIGENOUS LITERACIES

The Indigenous peoples of the North American continent spoke hundreds of languages. In addition to the spoken word, their communication methods include petroglyphs, wampum belts, and books with symbols painted on bark cloth.

Because these are not alphabetic methods of communication, they are often dismissed as evidence that Indigenous peoples were "primitive," but they are, in fact, far from primitive. Such methods are increasingly used today. Consider symbols like "the golden arches" or emoticons and all the information they tell you.

Indigenous languages differ from English or other European languages, both in their structure and in some of the sounds used. Maskoke, the language spoken by the Muscogee people, is one example. The written alphabet that was developed for Maskoke in the 1800s uses letters that look like those in the English alphabet,

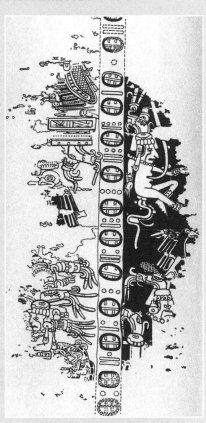

Mayan society had a system of writing that used glyphs, drawings, and other symbols. Those who could read and write kept records of religious, scientific, and cultural information, as well as stories, in bark cloth books now called codexes. The image above is from one of the few remaining codexes. Spanish invaders burned the others.

(continues on next page)

but some represent different sounds. The symbol V represents an "uh" sound and the K represents a sound between the English K and hard G. The Muscogee name for the squatters in their Georgia homelands was ekvnv vnoksulke ("people greedily grasping after the land"). Some English speakers spelled it "ecunnaunuxulgee."

English speakers who tried to write words from Indigenous languages did not always agree on how to spell them. That is why you might see "Muscogee" or "Muskogee," as well as "Maskoke," on highway or street signs where Muscogee people live; it's the same word but with different spellings.

In about 1809 a Cherokee man named Sequoyah developed a written form of the Cherokee language. The characters he created represented syllables rather than letter sounds, so it is called a syllabary rather than an alphabet. Many Cherokees gradually began to use this written form of their language. The newspaper the *Cherokee Phoenix* is one example. People who teach and speak the Cherokee language today use Sequoyah's syllabary.

In chapter 9 you will read about boarding schools created by the US government. One of its goals was to eradicate Indigenous languages. The schools led to a marked decrease in use of Indigenous languages, but in recent years, Indigenous people have been working on language revitalization programs. If you like to learn different languages, you may find some of these programs by searching online, using "language revitalization" plus "Indigenous" to do your search. One name that you can use to conduct this search is Esther Martinez. Her work on language revitalization led Congress to pass the Native American Languages Preservation Act. She was from Ohkay Owingeh, one of the Pueblo nations in the Southwest.

Squatters were also encroaching on Cherokee lands. After settler forces defeated the Cherokees in 1776, one group of Cherokees strongly opposed to ceding any more land moved farther west. They settled near present-day Chattanooga, Tennessee, near the Chickamauga Creek, and came to be known as the Chickamaugas. The back-country squatters viewed the Chickamaugas as a serious threat. In 1784 some of those settlers, led by John Sevier, seceded from North Carolina in the hope of creating a fourteenth state, which they named Franklin. Neither North Carolina nor the US government recognized its bid for statehood, but they lacked the resources to force Franklin back into North Carolina's control. Under Sevier's leadership, Franklin continued to encroach on Chickamauga lands. Ignoring Sevier's wishes, in 1785 the Cherokee and the US negotiated the Hopewell Treaty, which was supposed to keep non-Indigenous settlers east of the Blue Ridge Mountains.

It seems likely that the US government knew that the squatters would not abide by the treaty. Indeed, thousands of squatters had already claimed nearly a million acres of land west of the mountains. The Washington administration gave the appearance of wanting to treat tribal nations fairly, but its actions spoke otherwise. Secretary of War Knox advised the squatters' leaders to continue building in order to attract more illegal settlers. He seemed to ignore that settlers were provoking the Indigenous peoples, who were well aware of what the settlers intended. In 1788 war broke out between the Chickamaugas and the Franklin settlers and continued for several years.

Faced with ongoing Indigenous resistance and continuous pressure from settlers, Washington's administration negotiated the first of many treaties it would make with Indigenous nations. Unlike previous treaties, these would be ratified by the new Congress of the United States.

The first of these treaties, the Treaty of New York, was negotiated with representatives of the Muscogee Nation in 1790. The treaty stated that in exchange for vast swaths of Muscogee land that would become part of what is now Georgia, the US government would pay $1,500 each year to the Muscogee Nation. The agreement canceled treaties the Muscogee had made with the Georgia state government and with Spain. It also stated that any person "not being an Indian" who tried to settle or hunt on Muscogee lands would not be protected by the United States.

However, squatters ignored the treaty's provisions and tried to provoke the Muscogees to war. They slaughtered hundreds of deer in the Muscogee deer parks with the intention of destroying a primary source of food and income. The War Department also violated terms of the Treaty of New York. Officials bribed some Muscogee leaders, hoping to secure their loyalty. Such actions added to divisions within the Muscogee Nation, damaging the traditional decision-making processes and leaving the Muscogee vulnerable to betrayals of trust in leadership.

The Cherokee Nation also gave up territory in treaties with the US government during that time period. In July 1791 they reluctantly signed the Treaty of Holston, agreeing to abandon any claims to land on which the Franklin settlements sat in return for an annual annuity of $1,000 from the federal government. The Chickamaugas did not consider the treaty legitimate and continued to resist Sevier and the Franklinites.

It soon became clear that the US had no intention of stopping settlers who violated treaties. Recognizing their mutual interest in keeping settlers off their remaining homelands, the Chickamaugas and Muscogees began fighting alongside each other in and around Franklin.

In April 1792 Knox wrote to James Seagrove, the Indian agent working with the Muscogees, asking him to advise the Muscogees not to fight. By then Knox was characterizing the Muscogees in two ways. He called those who were benefiting from the Treaty of New York a "respectable" class of Indians. He regarded those who rejected the treaty as a group of outlaws and claimed that their actions did not reflect the will of Muscogee leaders who signed the treaty. The "outlaw" group of Muscogees, led by Alexander McGillivray, took up arms and attacked settlers. That September one of the settlers

DID YOU KNOW?

What is sometimes called a "client class" developed in the southeastern Indigenous nations. An Indigenous client class is a group of individuals who gain certain privileges from the colonizers in exchange for their cooperation. This relatively small number of Indigenous peoples, often treated as an Indigenous "elite," adopted some of the values and practices of the colonizers. In the Southeast, some embraced the enslavement of Africans and a few even became wealthy planters. Such class divisions internally damaged the traditional, relatively egalitarian Indigenous societies. The damage was especially serious when the US government treated members of the client class as spokespersons who could be involved in peace negotiations on behalf of their nations. Some of those negotiations put money into the pockets of the client class and the colonizers at the expense of tribal citizens.

wrote to the South Carolina and US governments warning that if troops did not come defend them from Indigenous attacks, the settlers might ally with Spain.

In fall of 1792, under the leadership of Dragging Canoe and Cheeseekau (a brother of Tecumseh), a contingent of Chickamauga, Muscogee, and Shawnee fighters set out to attack frontier settlements in what is now Tennessee. They laid siege to Buchanan's Station outside Nashville for several days. After Cheeseekau was killed, they returned to their villages.

After the fight at Buchanan's Station, the settlers were certain that war against the Chickamaugas was necessary. William Blount, who had been involved in negotiating the Treaty of Holston, tried to persuade the Chickamaugas to stop fighting, warning that the frontier settlers were "always dreadful, not only to the warriors, but to the innocent and helpless women and children, and old men."[4]

Blount did not want the fighting to erupt into full-scale war. He knew, however, that the settlers were eager to destroy Chickamauga towns. In September 1792 he ordered Sevier to form a company of rangers to protect the frontier and guard settlements. He was to remain on the defensive. Blount also warned the settlers against attacking Indigenous towns. But in early 1793 he had to order the militia to break up a mob of three hundred settlers who were bent on starting a war. They were acting, he later wrote, out of a "mistaken zeal to serve their country."[5]

In Georgia, treaty violations by settlers continued, as did armed resistance and retaliation by some Muscogee fighters. In early 1793 federal Indian agent George Seagrove identified five Muscogee towns, consisting of about five hundred people in all, as the center of that resistance. He and Knox were concerned that the settlers would start slaughtering Muscogees at will. In April, Knox began recruiting "expert and hardy woodsmen" from the Georgia militia to be rangers in federal service, thinking this would keep Georgia from starting its own war.[6] Georgians, however, including Governor Edward Telfair, had little regard for federal authority. The governor told Knox that he would not be able to restrain his people from fighting the Muscogee.

Lack of respect for government authority was a major issue in the early days of the United States. In July 1793 Sevier circumvented Blount's authority and convinced the War Department to let him conduct reconnaissance in Chickamauga territory. He soon altered that mission. For the next year he and his rangers burned Indigenous fields and killed their livestock in an effort to end the resistance and take over the land.

Tension continued between Georgia and the federal government throughout 1793. By September the Georgia militia had orders to abduct anyone, American or Indigenous, who might be trying to make peace. Open threats of assassination were made against Seagrove, the Indian agent. Militias

CONSIDER THIS

You have seen that two secession movements have taken place, and in neither of those were the settlers who seceded killed or punished by the government. In fact, Sevier went on to become a governor, and there is a statue of him in the US Capitol. You have also seen that the Indigenous peoples' defense of their homelands was met with irregular warfare and deceit, even in the making of treaties. What might be some reasons for these two very different approaches on the part of the federal government?

attacked several Muscogee towns in the fall of 1793, with the obvious goal of provoking the Muscogee to fight back. Seagrove managed to avert open conflict by persuading Muscogee leaders to keep their young men from retaliating, convincing them that the majority of Georgians did not want war.

That winter Governor Telfair was replaced by George Mathews, a land speculator who saw that he could make more money if ownership of lands passed peacefully from Indigenous people to the settlers. But despite what Seagrove had told the Muscogees, some Georgians were still eager for war. In the spring of 1794 an armed group of Georgia border squatters tried to establish their own independent republic on the Oconee River. They were led by veteran Indian killer Elijah Clarke, who had been a general in the Georgia militia during the war for independence. Clarke's rebellion ended without bloodshed when he and his followers surrendered to state troops.

In fall 1794, 1,750 Franklin rangers attacked two Chickamauga villages, burning all the buildings and fields at harvesttime and shooting those who tried to flee. The Chickamaugas had difficulty withstanding these attacks and surrendered shortly afterward.

■　■　■

From 1780 to 1815 conflicts in the Ohio Country and farther south led to treaties through which Indigenous peoples lost their homelands. To Indigenous peoples, the treaties were about relationships. To the settlers, the treaties were transactions through which they acquired lands. In the southern states this land would often be turned into vast plantations of cash crops worked by enslaved African men, women, and children. To make more money, plantation owners needed to acquire still more land. They became wealthier, and that wealth helped fuel the US economy.

The push for more land and more wealth drove out settlers who had small farms or no land at all. They moved farther west, where they squatted on lands that belonged to other Indigenous peoples. Some settlers viewed the federal government as their enemy for not wiping out Indigenous peoples completely. They saw those who carried out irregular warfare, including themselves, as frontier heroes who embodied an American spirit, one that would, as time passed, be revered in statues and stories about the nation's early years.

Though Indigenous nations had already been forced to give up so much during the early days of the US, settlers wanted more, and they would get it in the coming years. Under the leadership of Andrew Jackson, federal forces would soon make it clear that the government would readily turn to genocidal policies, including forced removals of Indigenous peoples.

CHAPTER SIX

JEFFERSON, JACKSON, AND THE PURSUIT OF INDIGENOUS HOMELANDS

The Shawnee, Cherokee, and Muscogee were by no means the only Indigenous nations in the South and Ohio Country resisting settlers during the period from 1776 to 1812. Other nations, like the Choctaw and Chickasaw, also resisted, but throughout the first decades of the 1800s, they all lost territory to the US government.

The US increased its land base in other ways too. The largest acquisition took place in 1803, when Thomas Jefferson's administration purchased 828,000 square miles of North American land from France. This purchase doubled the size of the United States. As was the case with the Treaty of Paris, neither government consulted with the Native nations that the land belonged to, including the Sioux, Cheyenne, Arapaho, Crow, Pawnee, Osage, and Comanche. Eventually fifteen states would be partially or fully formed by territory from what would come to be known as the Louisiana Purchase: Arkansas, Colorado, Iowa, Kansas, Louisiana, Minnesota, Missouri, Montana, Nebraska, New Mexico, North and South Dakota, Oklahoma, Texas, and Wyoming. The United States now bordered more land occupied by Spain, which included

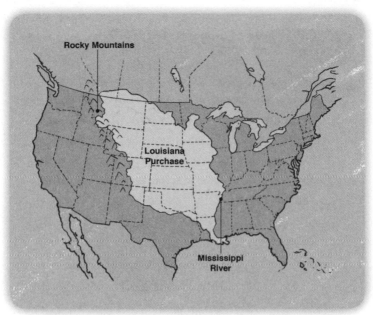

Indigenous people were not involved in the sale of the land that we know today as the Louisiana Purchase.

Texas and all the territory west of the Continental Divide to the Pacific Ocean.

The US government saw this purchase as a strategic means of averting war with France and gaining greater access to the Mississippi River as a trade route. The additional territory would be a boon to land speculators and would-be settlers. Though the land west of the Mississippi was already home to many Indigenous nations, the government would soon use it as a place to put other tribes they "removed" from their homelands.

Settlers' desire for large tracts of land to develop into plantations was an important factor leading to the removal of southern tribal nations: the Choctaw, Chickasaw, Cherokee, Muscogee, and Seminole.

You may recall the quote from Thomas Jefferson from chapter 4 about wanting to move Cherokees out of Georgia. Though Andrew Jackson is most often associated with removal of the southern Indigenous nations, he was implementing Jefferson's idea, and many of the actual removals would take place under Martin Van Buren's administration. This "exceptional" nation was, at its highest levels, engaging in what today is often called ethnic cleansing.

CONSIDER THIS

You may have heard the term *ethnic cleansing* in news stories about conflicts in foreign countries. The term came into use during the twentieth century. The United Nations has two definitions:

> Rendering an area ethnically homogeneous by using force or intimidation to remove persons of given groups from the area.[1]

And

> A purposeful policy designed by one ethnic or religious group to remove by violent and terror-inspiring means the civilian population of another ethnic or religious group from certain geographic areas.[2]

Bringing a critical lens to words we use is important. Generally speaking, people think of cleansing as a good; the removal of something bad or dirty. But people are not bad, dirty objects that can be removed or done away with, without regard for their humanity. The term *cleansing* hides the motives and actions of powerful governments or groups who are deliberately harming many people. What other terms can you think of that might be more accurate?

People in the US tend to think of past presidents as heroic. There is danger in romanticizing any person, but especially ones who, like Thomas Jefferson and Andrew Jackson, acquired wealth and status by taking actions that directly or indirectly harmed others.

Jefferson was born in 1743 on his family's plantation in Shadwell, Virginia. His parents' families had been among the earliest British colonizers, arriving in the 1600s. In spite of having little formal education, his father Peter Jefferson became a land surveyor who was recognized as a "frontier hero" for making an accurate map of the Colony of Virginia. Peter Jefferson died when Thomas was fourteen years old. The boy then helped his mother run the plantation. As a young man he attended the College of William and Mary. He studied law and was admitted to the Virginia bar in 1767.

As the wealthy owner of a plantation worked by enslaved Africans, Jefferson was well positioned to play key roles in the formation of the United States. He became president in 1801 and served two terms. As a political leader, he was determined to achieve status and expand the United States by taking lands that belonged to Native peoples and encouraging settlement by white Americans.

Andrew Jackson was born in 1767 in a Scotch-Irish community on the North Carolina border with South Carolina. His parents had arrived in North America in 1765 in one of the waves of Ulster Scots who left Ireland and colonized Indigenous homelands.

Jackson studied law and passed the bar exam in 1787, twenty years after Jefferson. He practiced law in North Carolina and later in Tennessee. He got involved in politics and briefly represented Tennessee in the US

Senate. After only a few months he left the Senate in 1798 to serve several years as a judge for the state's highest court. In 1801 he was appointed colonel in the Tennessee militia. He would spend many years as a commander of both state and federal forces whose main goal was to take over the homelands of Indigenous peoples. He became president in 1829 and served two terms.

Both Jefferson and Jackson owned plantations that would not have succeeded without enslaved laborers, both had served in a state militia, and both were intent on taking land from Indigenous peoples. Jefferson's weapon was political; he crafted policies that gave settlers the clear impression that it was all right to use and take Indigenous lands. Jackson's weapon was more literal. With his militias and the US military he took the lands by force.

Some people think of these two men as heroic. Native peoples think otherwise.

INDIGENOUS RESISTANCE TO DISHONEST DEALINGS

In the Southeast, the new US republic made it very hard for Indigenous tribes to continue trading with the Spanish in Florida. Tribes were forced to trade exclusively with US traders and were soon deeply in debt. The only way out was to cede land.

This was no accidental outcome.

The conditions for it were created and encouraged by Thomas Jefferson and others who were determined to get Indigenous lands. In 1803 Jefferson outlined a policy that described how the government would cheat Indigenous nations out of their land. First, the government would encourage settlement in and around Indigenous territory, preventing Indigenous people from hunting there. This would force them to take up agriculture and to go into debt buying the equipment they needed.

In a letter to William Henry Harrison in 1803, Thomas Jefferson wrote that he would

> be glad to see the good & influential individuals among them run in debt, because we observe that when these debts get beyond what the individuals can pay, they become willing to lop [them] off by a cession of lands.[3]

The effectiveness of Jefferson's scheme is evident in treaties the Choctaws and Chickasaws made two years after his letter to Harrison. In 1805 the Choctaws ceded most of their lands to the United States for $50,500 (worth approximately $1,088,300 in 2018), and the Chickasaws relinquished all their lands north of the Tennessee River for $20,000. Many Choctaws and Chickasaws became landless and were burdened by debts and poverty.

Even though many Indigenous nations east and southeast of the Mississippi had lost most of their territories, Indigenous resistance to the takeover continued. One site of that resistance was the Muscogee Nation.

There was tension between two groups within the Muscogee Nation. The Lower Creeks were willing to become more like the settlers, and the Upper Creeks wanted to maintain their cultural traditions. The Lower Creeks gradually went into debt as they purchased items to farm their private landholdings and became economically dependent on the settlers. This was largely due to diligent work by veteran US Indian agent Benjamin Hawkins. In 1796 George Washington had appointed him to work with the Muscogees and other tribes south of the Ohio River. His assignment was to persuade them to adopt European American values and practices. Hawkins worked primarily with Lower Creeks, leaving the Upper Creeks alone.

Over several years tension built between the traditionalists and those who accepted European American ideas. Conflict erupted into civil war within the Muscogee Nation in 1813 when traditionalist fighters called Red Sticks began an offensive against anyone associated with Hawkins's program. Part of their strategy was to kill Muscogee Nation livestock, both to deprive US soldiers of food and to rid Muscogee culture of the colonizers' influence. The chaos they created provoked a genocidal counterattack by Andrew Jackson's Tennessee militia. Jackson's goal was extermination of the entire Muscogee Nation.

Allies of the Red Sticks included Shawnee fighters and Africans who had freed themselves from slavery. In 1813 they set up a fortified encampment with their families at Tohopeka at Horseshoe Bend on the Tallapoosa River in present-day Alabama. Jackson mobilized a force of six hundred Lower Creek and Cherokee allies and seven hundred mounted militiamen and attacked the Red Stick stronghold in March 1814. The mercenaries captured three hundred Red Stick wives and children and held them as hostages to force a Muscogee surrender. Of a thousand Red Sticks and allies, eight hundred were killed. Jackson lost forty-nine men.

In the aftermath of the Battle of Horseshoe Bend, as it is known in most history textbooks, Jackson's troops

RED STICK
FORTIFICATIONS AT TOHOPEKA

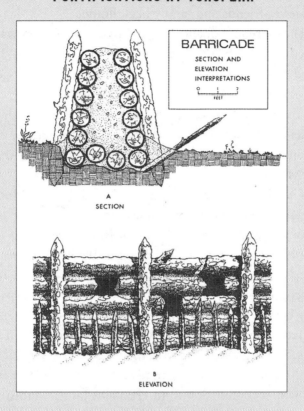

The Red Sticks and their allies built an elaborate fortification around their encampment. Its complexity surprised Jackson and continues to impress historians. A government document published in 1815 indicates that the wall was made of two rows of heavy logs, ranging in height from five to eight feet. Between the two rows, the builders had packed clay. Cannonballs the troops fired at it were either buried in the wall or bounced off.

mutilated the bodies of those they killed at Tohopeka. Their grotesque actions included using skin from bodies to make horses' bridles and sending "souvenirs" from corpses to friends and family back home.

The surrender document the Muscogee Nation was forced to sign was the Treaty with the Creeks, 1814. It ceded more than twenty-two million acres of Muscogee homeland to the United States and forced surviving Muscogees to move onto western remnants of their lands. Muscogee Nation territory now lay open to settlers; within a few years it would become the states of Alabama and Mississippi.

The first paragraph of the treaty says that the Muscogees had lost under "principles of national justice and honorable war." The mutilation of Muscogee bodies negates any claims of a just or honorable war, as does the treaty's abandonment of the small group of Lower Creek Muscogee who had fought alongside Jackson's troops. They begged Jackson to spare them and their holdings, but Jackson did not relent. "We bleed our enemies in such cases," he explained, "to give them their senses."[4] Jackson, far from being reprimanded for his genocidal methods, won a commission from President James Madison to become major general in the US Army.

When the Creek War ended, some of the Red Sticks joined the Seminole Nation in the Florida Everglades. The Indigenous peoples who are known today as Seminoles originally lived in towns along rivers in a large area that included what is now the Florida Panhandle. Born of resistance, the Seminole Nation included refugees from dozens of distinct Indigenous communities and Africans who had escaped slavery.

In 1817 the US entered the first of its three wars with the Seminole Nation. The First Seminole War (1817–1819) began when US authorities entered Spanish Florida illegally to recover US plantation owners' "property": people who had escaped slavery. The Seminoles repelled the invasion. Then, in 1818, President James Monroe ordered Major General Andrew Jackson to lead three thousand soldiers into Florida to crush the Seminoles and recapture anyone who had taken refuge from slavery there. His forces destroyed a number of Seminole settlements but could not destroy the Seminole resistance, and the Seminoles foiled the attempt to force people back to the plantations where they had been enslaved.

The Seminoles were never conquered and never signed a treaty with the United States. Although some were forcibly removed to Oklahoma in 1832, the Seminole Nation has never ceased to exist in the Everglades.

■ JACKSON'S MOVES TOWARD ETHNIC CLEANSING

Upon Jackson's election as president, the Georgia legislature claimed most of the Cherokee Nation's land, resolved that the Cherokee constitution and laws were null and void, and declared Cherokees subject to Georgia law. The Cherokee Nation objected and took their case against Georgia to the US Supreme Court. In 1829, while the case was working its way through the legal system, gold was discovered in Georgia. Forty thousand gold seekers ran roughshod over Cherokee lands. Shortly after that, the Supreme Court heard another case regarding the Cherokee Nation. In both cases the Court affirmed that state laws could not invalidate laws of an Indigenous nation that was under the protection of the United States because of their treaty relationship.

But Jackson, who as president was sworn to uphold those treaties, showed no concern for protecting the rights of the Cherokees or any other tribal nation. He was mainly interested in removing all Indigenous peoples across the Mississippi River.

POLITICAL RHETORIC

It is important to learn how to interpret the political rhetoric of government officials. They often say one thing but mean something else entirely.

Let's do a critical analysis of what President Andrew Jackson said in a message to Congress in 1829 about Removal:

> The emigration should be voluntary, for it would be as cruel as unjust to compel the aborigines to abandon the graves of their fathers and seek a home in a distant land. But they should be distinctly informed that, if they remain within the limits of the States, they must be subject to their laws. In return for their obedience, as individuals, they will, without doubt, be protected in the enjoyment of those possessions which they have improved by their industry.

Settlers hearing Jackson's words would think he was a good guy. We imagine they might think this:

> We aren't going to be cruel to the Indian people! We're good Americans! We care about them. But if they're going to stay east of the Mississippi, they have to stop being Indians and start being Americans. And they gotta follow our laws. If they do that, they can keep their houses and farms and cows or whatever. But if they won't, they gotta go.

A Native person might react this way to Jackson's speech:

> We've heard this before. He will change his mind tomorrow. He might not even mean it today! It wouldn't be the first time these American leaders pretended to care about our lives then deceived us. He says we must either leave our homes and the graves of our ancestors or live as farmers without the protection of our own people, among settlers who are likely to attack us as soon as the soldiers aren't looking. My white neighbors know that farming means going into debt. And staying here means that we cease to exist as nations. But to go West, away from our homes, our lands, to try to make new lives? This is the cruelest choice we have ever been forced to make.

Jackson's political rhetoric, using words like "voluntary emigration," was meant to disguise his true intent. His Removal policy fits the United Nations definition of ethnic cleansing.

President Jackson worked with Congress to ratify the Indian Removal Act. Passed in 1830, it authorized the government to create tracts of land west of the Mississippi to be assigned to specific tribes and to enter into new treaties. These new treaties would cede Indigenous homelands to the United States in exchange for that new land base across the Mississippi. When leaders of the Cherokee Nation resisted signing a new treaty, agents of the US government held them in jail and closed their printing press. With the leaders jailed, the US negotiated with Cherokees who had no authorization to represent the Cherokee Nation. In the end, Jackson got the signed agreements he needed as a cover for forced removal.

Most textbooks that talk about removals use the term Trail of Tears and focus only on the Cherokee Nation. In fact, the outcome of the Removal Act was many Trails of Tears.

Following passage of the act, the United States made eighty-six treaties with twenty-six Indigenous nations located between New York and the Mississippi. All the treaties coerced the nations into ceding land and led to forced removals. Within some nations, such as the Kickapoo, contingents of people left the United States and fled to Canada or Mexico. One Indigenous leader who resisted removal was Black Hawk of the Sauk Nation.

Believing that the Sauk territory had not been ceded in a lawful way, in 1832 Black Hawk led a group of his people from present-day Iowa back onto their homelands in Illinois. The settlers there assumed they were being invaded. Illinois militia and federal troops responded, killing many Sauks over a four-month period. The outcome of what is called the Black Hawk War was the removal of the Sauks to a reservation for the Sauk and Fox in Iowa.

Following the Treaty of the Cherokee Agency in 1817 some Cherokees left their homelands for land in what is now the state of Arkansas. A larger group left in 1832, but most remained on what was left of their territory. Before and after the Removal Act was passed, leaders of the Cherokee Nation wrote several letters to Congress protesting Removal and asking Congress to honor the treaties it had made with them. Their letters were unsuccessful. In 1838 the forced march of the Cherokee Nation began. Now known as the Trail of Tears, it was an arduous journey from remaining Cherokee homelands in

Georgia and Alabama to what would later become north-eastern Oklahoma.

After the Civil War, journalist James Mooney interviewed people who had been involved in the forced removal. Based on these firsthand accounts, he described events of 1838 when the US Army removed the last of the Cherokees by force:

> Squads of troops were sent to search out with rifle and bayonet every small cabin hidden away in the coves or by sides of mountain streams, to seize and bring in as prisoners all the occupants, however or wherever they might be found. Families at dinner were startled by the sudden gleam of bayonets in the doorway and rose up to be driven with blows and oaths along the weary miles of trail that led to the stockade. Men were seized in their fields or going along the road, women were taken from their wheels and children from their play. In many cases, on turning for one last look as they crossed the ridge, they saw their homes in flames, fired by the lawless rabble that followed on the heels of the soldiers to loot and pillage. So keen were these outlaws on the scene that in some instances they were driving off the cattle and other stock of the Indians almost before the soldiers had fairly started their owners in the other direction. Systematic hunts were made by the same men for Indian graves, to rob them of the silver pendants and other valuables deposited with the dead. A Georgia volunteer, afterward a colonel in the Confederate service, said: "I fought through the civil war and have seen men shot to pieces and slaughtered by thousands, but the Cherokee removal was the cruelest work I ever knew."[5]

Half of the sixteen thousand Cherokee men, women, and children who were rounded up and force-marched in the dead of winter perished on the journey out of their country.

The Muscogees and Seminoles suffered similar death rates in their forced removal. A great many Chickasaws and Choctaws died too. The French political scientist Alexis de Tocqueville wrote about what he observed as a large group of Choctaws prepared to cross the Mississippi River at Memphis in 1831:

> It was then the middle of winter, and the cold was unusually severe; the snow had frozen hard upon the ground, and the river was drifting huge masses of ice. The Indians had their families with them; and they brought in their train the wounded and sick, with children newly born, and old men upon the verge of death. They possessed neither tents nor wagons, but only their arms and some provisions. I saw them embark to pass the mighty river, and never will that solemn spectacle fade from my remembrance. No cry, no sob was heard amongst the assembled crowd; all were silent. Their calamities were of ancient date, and they knew them to be irremediable. The Indians had all stepped into the bark which was to carry them across, but their dogs remained upon the bank. As soon as these animals perceived that their masters were finally leaving the shore, they set up a dismal howl, and, plunging all together into the icy waters of the Mississippi, they swam after the boat.[6]

■ ■ ■

At the time of US independence, most of the 2.5 to 4 million Europeans who became Americans were living within fifty miles of the Atlantic Ocean. In the next half century, in one of the largest and most rapid migrations in world history, over four million settlers would cross the Appalachians. The ideas of Thomas Jefferson and the actions of Andrew Jackson made it possible for the United States to grow as an empire on a single continent.

The takeover of Indigenous homelands did not end with the removal of Eastern tribes to the "Indian Territories" west of the Mississippi. Every Indigenous nation on the continent eventually dealt with settlers who, with the help of the US government, were bent on its destruction, removal, or assimilation. James Monroe's administration established the Office of Indian Affairs in the Department of War in 1824. At the time, that department was responsible for negotiating treaties that were intended to bring about an end to warfare between the US and Indigenous nations. Twenty-five years later the office was transferred to the Department of the Interior. This happened after the US and Mexico signed the Treaty of Guadalupe Hidalgo, which added over five-hundred-thousand square miles of land that would become the states of Arizona, California, Nevada, Utah, and parts of Colorado, New Mexico, and Wyoming. This move suggests that government officials believed armed Indigenous resistance would no longer be a problem.

They were mistaken.

CHAPTER SEVEN

SEA TO SHINING SEA

Thomas Jefferson and other political leaders of his day envisioned a country that spanned the continent from one coast to the other. If you have sung "America the Beautiful," you have used the metaphor "from sea to shining sea" to describe the United States. In reality, Indigenous peoples had already connected the Pacific and the Atlantic Seaboards with networks of diplomacy and cultural exchange, predating Jefferson's idea by several thousand years. To achieve the goal Jefferson articulated, the fledgling United States would have to invade and occupy lands west of the Mississippi.

Before their encounters with the United States, the Native people there had fought invasion and occupation by Spain, and they contended with colonizers from Mexico after it won independence from Spain.

This chapter will look at the experiences of the Indigenous peoples of what we know today as the southwestern United States: Arizona, California, Colorado, New Mexico, Texas, and Utah.

■ INDIGENOUS RESISTANCE TO SPANISH AND MEXICAN OCCUPATION

In the early 1500s Spain laid claim to the vast lands of what is now the southwestern US, calling the region

Nueva España (New Spain). It may be helpful to remember that Europeans created the Doctrine of Discovery to justify their takeover of any territory they "discovered" regardless of whose home it was. From an Indigenous perspective, European claims to Indigenous lands were not legitimate. In the Discovery Doctrine mind-set, what Indigenous peoples thought about it was irrelevant.

New Spain included the homelands of the Apaches, Caddos, Comanches, Miwoks, Navajos, Pueblos, Utes, and many other nations. Some of these Indigenous groups lived in communities along the Gulf of Mexico or on the Pacific Coast or built towns and farms along major rivers in desert areas. Other groups were more mobile, purposefully traveling from one location to another as dictated by availability of game, water, and other resources. These peoples spoke hundreds of languages but were all part of the extensive Indigenous trading networks that connected the peoples of the Pacific and the Atlantic Seaboards. When disagreements over resources evolved into warfare, they also relied on diplomacy to resolve the conflicts.

Throughout northern New Spain, the Spanish occupation involved the military, the Catholic Church, miners, and settlers. Spanish troops protected the missions, the settlers, and the mining operations from Indigenous resistance to occupation and exploitation of their homelands. The missionaries were there to convert Indigenous peoples to Christianity, but they also wanted their forced labor to support the missions and the Crown. Spain intended to make all Indigenous peoples dependent on trade with Spain for their survival regardless of whether they were part of the Catholic missions. The Spanish also used diplomacy, including treaties and less formal agreements, which allowed them to use Indigenous land and other resources in exchange for food, horses, livestock, and other trade items.

INDIGENOUS PEOPLES OF WHAT ARE NOW CALLED ARIZONA AND NEW MEXICO

By the late sixteenth century CE, Indigenous people in what is currently Arizona, Colorado, New Mexico, and Utah—including Apaches and Navajos—were living in more than one hundred communities and in ninety-eight interrelated city-states that included Hopi, Zuni, Taos, Picuris, and Nambé.

When the Spanish invaded the area in 1598, they used the word *pueblos* (towns) to describe these Indigenous city-states, and eventually the word also came to refer to the people themselves. The Pueblo Indians had a thriving irrigation-based system of agriculture and highly developed religions. The Spanish assault on the Pueblo peoples was brutal. Within two decades they had destroyed most of the Pueblo towns and enslaved the people. With the military's support, Franciscan missionaries forbade Pueblos' religious practices and forced them to convert to Christianity. Pueblo resistance to the Spanish was ongoing.

In 1680 the religious leader Po'pay led a well-planned revolt. This revolution was supported by the Navajos, Apaches, and Utes and was joined by captive Indigenous and mestizo servants and laborers in the Spanish capital at Santa Fe. (Mestizos are people of mixed racial heritage, usually Indigenous and Spanish.)

The Pueblo forces and their allies drove the Spanish out of the region, leaving the Pueblos free for twelve years. Then the Spanish invaded again and recolonized that area.

For the next 130 years Spain maintained strict control over the Pueblos and forced them to provide foot soldiers for Spanish forays against other Indigenous nations. Mexican independence in 1821 ended Spanish persecution of the Pueblos, but by that time the colonizers had taken over much of the Pueblo homelands.

This statue of Po'pay stands in Emancipation Hall in the US Capitol Visitor Center. Designed and sculpted by Cliff Fragua of Jemez Pueblo, it is the only statue in the collection created by a Native artist. It was installed in 2005 as part of the National Statuary Hall Collection that was established by law on July 2, 1864. That law said that each state would provide two statues of significant people in the state's history.

INDIGENOUS PEOPLES OF WHAT IS NOW TEXAS

The Indigenous peoples of what is now Texas included those who lived along the Gulf Coast, like the Caddos, and those whose homelands were inland, like the Apache, Comanche, and Kiowa.

Their contact with Europeans likely began in 1528, when a Spanish expedition landed on the Gulf Coast west of the Mississippi River delta. Almost two hundred years would pass before the Spanish moved to occupy some of the most remote places in the region. In 1718 they established San Antonio, their first town in Texas, and Franciscan missionaries founded the Mission San Antonio de Valero (what we know today as the Alamo).

Maintaining peaceful relations with some Indigenous peoples, such as the Apaches and the Comanches, was never easy or certain for Spain throughout its occupation. When Mexico gained independence from Spain, it attempted to continue the diplomacy Spain had established with Indigenous peoples. This became too expensive for the overextended new nation, and before long Mexico was not honoring its agreements. In response, Apaches raided settlements in several northern Mexican states. Comanches and Kiowas also dramatically escalated their campaigns against settlers during the 1830s and 1840s, eventually attacking in the central states of Durango, Zacatecas, and San Luis Potosí.

The violence claimed thousands of settler and Indigenous lives while ruining much of northern Mexico's economy. This warfare seriously weakened the Mexican government and may have compromised its ability to fight when the United States declared war in 1846.

INDIGENOUS PEOPLES OF WHAT IS NOW CALLED CALIFORNIA

The Indigenous peoples of what is now California included the Chumash, Costanoan, Esselen, Gabrieliño, Kumeyaay, Luiseño, Miwok, Ohlone, Salinan, and Wappo.

Spain claimed these lands in the 1520s but did not begin the process of colonizing them until some 250 years later. To replenish some of its resources, including silver, and to fend off other European powers, the Spanish Crown began moving troops, settlers, and missionaries into what is now California in 1769. The Franciscan friar Junipero Serra established the mission of San Diego later that year. Many other missions followed, all protected by military installations called presidios.

Between 1769 and 1823, twenty-one Franciscan missions were established along a north-south road the Spanish called El Camino Real, which spanned more than five hundred miles in western California. The Camino Real served the interests of the military, the settlers, the miners, and the missionaries. Serra himself traveled between missions with soldiers to kidnap unsuspecting Indigenous individuals and families and take them to the nearest mission to be made into Christian converts and laborers. He recorded these captures in his diaries:

> [When] one fled from between their [the soldiers'] hands, they caught the other. They tied him, and it was all necessary, for even bound he defended himself that they should not bring him and flung himself on the ground with such violence that he scraped and bruised his thighs and knees. But at last they brought him. . . . He was most frightened and very disturbed.[1]

The violence these Indigenous people experienced did not end with their capture. Accounts from that time show repeatedly why so many "mission Indians" escaped when they could. Mission life was brutal. Analyses of the bones at the mission burial sites that compare them with bones found elsewhere show that the bones of those who died at the missions were stunted and smaller than the others.

DID YOU KNOW?

Teachers usually present the Spanish missions as places where Indigenous people were treated well and where they accepted Christianity. In textbooks and in many award-winning children's books, the history of the Catholic missions and Junipero Serra are shown as heroic and good. Indigenous peoples in California are pushing schools to change the ways that the history of the missions is taught to children so that students learn what really happened.

When the Catholic Church decided to make Serra a saint, Indigenous peoples of California asked to meet with the pope to ask him to revisit that decision. He did not, and in 2015, Serra became a saint of the Catholic Church.

Conditions for Indigenous people at the missions were notorious, but time and again, when European observers and Spanish officials objected, the Franciscans made no changes.

In 1775 a force of over six hundred Indigenous people from fifteen villages close to the San Diego Mission launched an organized attack on it, burning it to the ground. Officials at every mission feared similar organized assaults and uprisings. Spanish troops protected the missions until 1779 when the colonial government's emphasis shifted to creating, supporting, and protecting secular towns rather than missions.

Spain's empire in the Americas was gradually coming apart. Indigenous peoples were playing key roles in independence movements in South America and the Caribbean in the early 1800s. In 1810 Father Miguel Hidalgo, a priest who was deeply involved with Indigenous communities in Mexico, led a revolt that culminated in Mexico's independence in 1821. The majority of the movement's fighters were drawn from Indigenous nations.

The new Republic of Mexico was unstable and impoverished as it emerged in 1821 from Spanish colonialism and a war of national liberation. It immediately opened its borders to trade, something Spanish authorities had never allowed.

US COLONIZATION OF NORTHERN MEXICO

The territory that became the states of Texas, New Mexico, Arizona, Utah, Nevada, Colorado, and California was in the sights of the US long before Mexico's independence from Spain. In 1806, during Thomas Jefferson's administration, army lieutenant Zebulon Pike was ordered to take a small force into Spanish-occupied territory to gather information that could later be used for military invasion. In essence, Pike was a spy gathering information, much like Lewis and Clark did on their "expedition." Pretending to have gone astray, Pike and his contingent built a fort on Spanish-occupied land in what is today called southern Colorado. Spanish authorities took them into custody and transported them to Chihuahua, Mexico. This arrest was apparently part of Pike's goal. He and his men were able to make notes about the Spanish presence in the region. After their eventual release, he compiled those notes into a book. Published in

1810, *The Expeditions of Zebulon Montgomery Pike* was a bestseller.

Before the publication of Pike's book, merchants in the United States had shown little interest in trading in Mexico. His account of the lucrative Indigenous network trading in furs and silver there changed their thinking. There was money to be made, and they moved to take over that trade.

These traders would help pave the way for the US to take political control of northern Mexico. Among them were US citizens like Christopher Houston "Kit" Carson, who married into the wealthy Spanish families there. Such marriages created strong alliances between the traders and the Spanish, which made it easier for them to control the lucrative trade in furs with Indigenous and other trappers.

Settlers from the US also began making inroads into Mexican territory through Mexico's land grant system. Starting in 1823, the Mexican government granted land in what is now Texas to agents who were required to recruit a minimum of two hundred families to settle the grant. During the first decade of Mexican independence, some thirty thousand settlers poured into the province from the United States.

St. Louis became a key city for trade into northern Mexico. It was connected to transatlantic trading companies in cities on the East Coast and had access to better quality goods than the Mexican ports. Many routes used for this trade were those Indigenous trade routes discussed in chapter 2. In 1825 the US Congress authorized the surveying of a trade route connecting Missouri with towns in northern Mexico. What became known as the Santa Fe Trail crossed through homelands of the Apache,

Arapaho, Cheyenne, Comanche, Jicarilla Apache, Kaw, Kiowa, Pawnee, and Pueblo peoples. Congress entered into treaties with some of these nations, such as the Osage, to allow traders to cross their land. Indigenous people who objected to the traders' presence on their homelands would often interfere with their passage, sometimes attacking them. In 1829, the first year of Jackson's presidency, the US began providing armed military escorts for the merchants and their cargo.

Although Mexico banned slavery in 1829, many of its land grants in the province of Texas were given to plantation owners from the US who used enslaved workers. Historians commonly refer to them as Anglo-Americans. They pressured Mexico to reverse the ban on slavery and to change other policies for the settlers. Over several years tensions grew and sometimes violence erupted. Eventually a group of these wealthy settlers developed a plot to have Texas secede from Mexico. The plot evolved into a war that included the famous 1836 Battle of the Alamo. The Anglo-American forces lost that battle, but within a month won the decisive battle at San Jacinto, and Mexico gave up the province of Texas. That conflict laid the groundwork for the US invasion of Mexico.

Several expeditions by Anglo-Americans into the Mexican territory that is now California and Oregon also helped pave the way for the United States to invade. Much as Zebulon Pike did decades earlier, Captain John C. Frémont and his guide Kit Carson set out to gather information that would aid military conquest. Some of these expeditions, like Pike's, were not legal and were troubling to Mexican authorities. For example, in 1846, Frémont entered the Sacramento Valley at a time when talk of war was growing louder. He promised military protection to Anglo-American settlers if they would side with the United States, should it declare war on Mexico.

Later that year, the US did just that. Military actions took place in the northern states of Mexico and along the Pacific and Gulf Coasts. US forces fought their way from Mexico's main commercial port of Veracruz on the Gulf of Mexico to the capital, Mexico City, nearly three hundred miles inland. The US Army occupied the capital until the Mexican government signed the Treaty of Guadalupe Hidalgo in 1848, ceding its northern territories, almost half of the territory it had occupied after independence from Spain. Like previous treaties between the US and other countries, the Treaty of Guadalupe Hidalgo was written and the new borders were drawn without any input from leaders of sovereign Native nations, as if their lives were of no consequence.

WRITING THE AMERICAN MYTH

The print media were useful in justifying why the United States was behaving like an imperial power despite its democratic ideals. For example, in an 1848 article about the war against Mexico, the editors of the influential *United States Magazine and Democratic Review* argued that the US was morally superior to Europe because European powers "conquer only to enslave," while the United States "conquers only to bestow freedom."[2] In reality, the US was a slaveholding nation that had not treated Indigenous peoples fairly before this war with Mexico and did not view Indigenous or Mexican people as equal to its white citizens. This article, like a great deal of writing of the early 1800s, was meant to justify, deny, or hide the nation's imperialism and genocidal actions. Many writers of the time, in fiction, nonfiction, and poetry, also insisted that the US was not the same kind of conqueror that European monarchies had been.

The novelist James Fenimore Cooper was among the first to provide a storyline that framed the country's beginnings as both fair and heroic. He is best known for his Leatherstocking Tales, including *The Last of the Mohicans*, which were published between 1823 and 1841. They feature the character Natty Bumppo, a British settler who is depicted as a friend of "the last Mohican," a fictional Delaware leader. Cooper's novels create a romantic myth of the country's birth, which begins with the French and Indian War and ends with settlement of the western plains. In Cooper's version of history, the last of the "noble" and "pure" Natives naturally die off to make way for Bumppo and people like him. This symbolically affirms the national idea that colonizers had a legitimate claim over what had been Indian land.

Cooper's Natty Bumppo was probably inspired by real-life colonizers such as Daniel Boone. Boone became a celebrity at age fifty in 1784 when real estate entrepreneur John Filson wrote and self-published *The Discovery, Settlement and Present State of Kentucke* to entice settlers to buy property from him in the Ohio Country. It included a map to guide illegal squatters through the region and a section titled "The Adventures of Col. Daniel Boone," supposedly written by Boone himself. That section included stories of his clashes with "bloodthirsty" Indians, and his "adventures" were later published in the *American Magazine* in 1787, then as a book. And so, a superstar was born: the mythical hero, hunter, and Indian fighter.

Daniel Boone is still seen as the kind of patriot who made America great. His popularity parallels that of *The Last of the Mohicans*, which was a bestseller throughout the nineteenth century and has never gone out of print. Boone and Bumppo are still featured in the curriculum in the US education system. Generations of readers who consume tales of Bumppo and Boone have interpreted them as fact, not fiction. In those stories, "frontiersmen" and "pioneers" are the heroes, while Indigenous peoples are enemies, or at least characterized as obstacles to the country's progress. The stories are not accurate, because they do not include Indigenous perspectives on invasion and colonization. Instead, they provide easy justification for centuries of assault on Indigenous peoples and help to ease any discomfort non-Native readers may feel about the reality of genocide.

Journalists and popular writers justified US efforts to take land from Mexico in the same way. For example, the poet Walt Whitman wrote during his time as a newspaper editor that "miserable, inefficient Mexico" could not possibly have any role in "the great mission of peopling the New World with a noble race." He claimed that it was "the law of the races" that "a superior grade of rats" would clear out "all the minor rats."[3] In other words, he believed that "Anglo-Saxons" would eliminate all the supposedly lesser races. When General Zachary Taylor's troops captured Monterrey in 1846, Whitman hailed it as "another clinching proof of the indomitable energy of the Anglo-Saxon character."[4]

In the five-year period leading up to, during, and immediately after the war with Mexico, many books were published that were strongly pro-war. A few writers openly opposed the war. Henry David Thoreau, John Greenleaf Whittier, and James Russell Lowell, for example, all favored abolition of slavery and did not want the US to turn Mexican territory into slaveholding states. At the same time, they believed that, as Lowell wrote, it was the destiny of "the English race" to occupy the entire continent.[5] Ralph Waldo Emerson, a pacifist who supported territorial expansion without war, also believed contact with the Mexican "race" would harm Americans.

It is important to note that none of these writers were critical of Manifest Destiny. Whether they were for or against the US war with Mexico, their writings reflected the established US origin myth that the frontier settlers must replace all others, including the Native peoples, on the continent.

■　■　■

With warfare and words, the United States had achieved Jefferson's goal of a country that spanned from the Atlantic to the Pacific Oceans. An unbroken line of states, however, would not exist until many years later because the US would grant statehood only when settlers in a territory outnumbered the Indigenous population. In the western part of the continent, this would soon fuel a push for increased settlement by white people, along with decimation or forced removal of Indigenous populations.

Even after the United States took over northern Mexico, Indigenous nations there, such as the Navajos,

Apaches, and Comanches, continued to resist the new regime, just as for centuries they had pushed back against colonization efforts by Spain and Mexico. The US Army sent regiments to protect settlers who crossed those Indigenous homelands to get to the northern California goldfields or the fertile valleys of the Pacific Northwest.

An America that spanned from "sea to shining sea" was not, in fact, as inevitable as stories of the Old West suggest. Why, then, does that idea persist? The answer is that few people, including very influential writers, question the idea that the United States was preordained by a higher power to fill the continent. That philosophy frames the invasions and occupations of Indigenous nations and Mexico not as imperialism or genocide but as progress toward fulfilling the country's destiny.

CHAPTER EIGHT

INDIGENOUS LANDS BECOME "INDIAN COUNTRY"

Filling the continent from sea to shining sea meant settling or squatting on Indigenous lands. By the eve of the Civil War, six of the seven departments of the US Army were stationed west of the Mississippi to protect those settlers and squatters. By depicting Indigenous peoples as savages at war with civilization, Americans were able to view the west as a violent place. To them, it was "Indian Country" that had to be "tamed" and be made theirs as quickly as possible.

President Abraham Lincoln was inaugurated in March 1861, two months after the South seceded from the Union. In 1862 he signed a set of laws that benefited land-poor settlers, gold prospectors, land speculators. The Homestead Act, the Pacific Railway Act, and the Morrill Act all took land from Indigenous peoples. Though they were hailed by land-hungry Americans as progress, in reality these laws were land grabs that undermined treaties the US had made with Indigenous nations.

The Civil War and the decades immediately after would see drastic changes in federal treaty making with Indigenous nations in addition to the slaughter to near extinction of the buffalo, a primary resource for the nations west of the Mississippi. In this chapter we will look closely at how events of that period affected Native nations and how they responded to increasing pressures from the United States.

INDIGENOUS NATIONS AND THE CIVIL WAR

When the Civil War broke out, some Indigenous people hoped for a victory for the Confederate States of America, which they believed would weaken the United States and stop its takeover of their homelands. The Indigenous nations most directly affected by the war were the Cherokee, Muscogee, Choctaw, Chickasaw, and Seminole. They had rebuilt their townships, farms, ranches, schools, and governments after their removal to Indian Territory. A tiny elite of each nation owned enslaved Africans and private estates and dominated their nations' politics. A majority of Indigenous people wanted to stay out of the fight between North and South. But when war broke out in 1861, these tribal governments, led by their wealthiest members, exercised their status as sovereign nations by signing treaties with the Confederacy.

Nearly seven thousand Cherokee, Muscogee, Choctaw, Chickasaw, and Seminole went into battle for the Confederacy. But a few months after the war broke out, thousands of volunteers from Indian Territory—mainly Indigenous men and self-emancipated African Americans—organized into regiments under the command of white officers to engage and harass the Confederate Army from Oklahoma to Kansas. During the war, many Indigenous soldiers who had begun the war fighting for the Confederacy became disillusioned and went over to the Union side.

Although in Indian Territory Union forces were getting help from Indigenous volunteers against the Confederacy, in other places Lincoln's army was at war with Indigenous peoples. For several decades, the federal government had been seizing territory that belonged to the Dakota people. In 1859 the United States turned some of their land into the state of Minnesota. Confined to reservations, the Dakota were no longer able to live and hunt freely on Minisota Makoce (Land Where the Waters Reflect the Skies or Heavens). By 1862 they were on the verge of starvation. Crops had failed and game was scarce. But most important, the federal government failed to meet many of its treaty obligations, including providing payments and supplies or keeping settlers from squatting on reservation lands.

When the Dakotas mounted an uprising to drive out the settlers, Union Army troops crushed the revolt. They rounded up thousands of men, women, children, and elders and held them at the Lower Sioux Agency in Morton, where they identified over three hundred who would be put on trial for murder. On November 7, 1862, those not destined for a courtroom in Mankato were marched over one hundred miles to Fort Snelling and imprisoned there. In Mankato, a commission of military officers heard the murder cases, sometimes reaching a verdict after only a few minutes. In all, 303 Dakota men were sentenced to death. After a review of the trial records, President Lincoln decided that thirty-nine of them should be executed. One was given a last-minute reprieve. On December 26, 1862, thirty-eight Dakota prisoners took their assigned places on a specially constructed scaffold. They grasped each others' hands and sang a Dakota song as they were hanged before some four thousand spectators.

It is the largest mass execution in US history.

As many as three hundred of the Dakota men, women, and children imprisoned at Fort Snelling died over the winter due to inhumane treatment and conditions. In May of 1863 those who survived were exiled to the Crow Creek Sioux Reservation in South Dakota.

When professional soldiers posted in the West were sent to fight the Confederacy, Lincoln called for volunteers to take their place keeping the peace, or in other words, to protect settlers, merchants, miners, and white travelers. Because these volunteer soldiers were paid by the federal government, their regiments were allowed to cross state and territorial boundaries. Volunteers came from many states and from territories that were seeking statehood. These territorial volunteer forces focused heavily on controlling or eliminating Indigenous civilian populations. The Lincoln administration did little or nothing to curb their vicious, genocidal actions against Native peoples.

Perhaps the most outrageous incident involving militias is the massacre at Sand Creek, carried out by the First and Third Colorado Volunteers. Their attack was led by John Chivington, a one-time Methodist pastor and an ambitious politician known as the "Fighting Parson."

Starting in June of 1864 groups of Cheyennes and Arapahos traveled to Fort Lyon in southeastern Colorado to avoid being considered hostile after attacks on settlers enraged the territory's white population. They camped by Sand Creek and were complying with all the conditions put on them by John Evans, the governor of the Colorado

Howling Wolf, a Cheyenne man who witnessed the Sand Creek Massacre, made this ledger art illustration of the attack in 1865. During the late 1800s, drawing in ledgers (similar to today's bound notebooks) gradually replaced painting on animal hides as a means for Native people to record events and depict stories of their lives.

Territory. But on November 29, Chivington and a force of seven hundred Colorado Volunteers attacked the camp without provocation or warning. They killed more than 130 women, children, and men and then scalped and mutilated the corpses, decorating their weapons and caps with body parts.

A congressional investigation heard detailed eyewitness reports of the soldiers' brutality. Horrified officials verbally condemned the attack and Chivington himself, but no one ever went to trial for the Sand Creek massacre.

The Volunteer Army of the Pacific led by US Army colonel James Carleton massacred hundreds of unarmed Shoshone, Bannock, and Ute people. Carleton also led a ruthless campaign against the Apaches. He was then promoted to brigadier general and spent the rest of the Civil War years engaged in a series of search-and-destroy missions against the Navajos. That campaign culminated in 1864 in series of forced removals during which some eight thousand Navajo civilians were marched more than three hundred miles to Fort Sumner, a military concentration camp at Bosque Redondo in what is currently eastern New Mexico. On the march and at the camp, conditions were brutal. Many Navajo people were killed, and many died of starvation.

Through it all, the Navajo people resisted Carleton's efforts to Christianize them and turn them against their traditional ways of life. In 1868 Navajo leaders signed a treaty with the US government, successfully negotiating

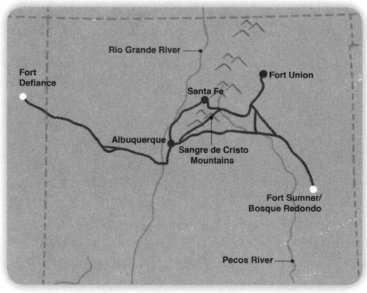

As this map shows, the Long Walk followed four different routes that ranged from 375 to 498 miles. Some routes went through mountains. All started at Fort Defiance and ended at Bosque Redondo, near Fort Sumner.

a return to their homelands in what is currently the Four Corners area of the southwestern United States.

INDIGENOUS PEOPLES AFTER THE CIVIL WAR

Having defeated the Confederate Army in 1865, the US Department of War rose in prestige. The armed forces were centralized under the president's command. The federal government focused its attention and its troop strength on Indigenous nations who challenged the US takeover of lands west of the Mississippi. Prominent Civil War officers led this charge, including William Tecumseh Sherman and George Armstrong Custer.

THE ALL-BLACK REGIMENTS IN THE US ARMY

In 1862 the Union Army began accepting free and formerly enslaved Africans as soldiers, but at lower pay and in segregated units under white officers. By the end of the Civil War in 1865, 186,000 black soldiers had fought and 38,000 had died in combat or from disease, a higher death toll than that of any individual state.

After the war many black soldiers, like their poor white counterparts, remained in the army. Army service gave them pay and a pension, and even some glory. The government had its own motives for assigning black troops to the West: whites in the East and the South did not want thousands of armed black soldiers in their communities. In 1866 Congress created six all-black regiments (later consolidated into four) that came to be known to the Native people of the West as Buffalo Soldiers. The Smithsonian's National Museum of African American History website states that there are differing theories for that nickname. But the soldiers considered the name itself to be high

(continues on next page)

praise because buffalo were deeply respected by Indigenous peoples of the Plains.

During the administration of President Ulysses S. Grant (1869–1877), the all-black regiments took part in some of the most intensive campaigns against Indigenous civilians.

This photograph of Buffalo Soldiers was taken by Christian Barthelmess, who was an official army photographer. Photographers of that period often carried studio props and had their subjects wear them. This made the subjects look authentic but was, in fact, a misrepresentation of the person being photographed.

After the Civil War, efforts to take land from Indigenous nations west of the Mississippi increased. Federal land grants to railroad barons stretched for dozens of miles on both sides of the railroad tracks and across Indigenous farms and hunting grounds. The US sent troops to protect the railroad companies and their workers and settlers who encroached on Indigenous lands. Soldiers and paid hunters began to attack the great buffalo herds.

For millennia, buffalo herds covered the Great Plains. Peoples of the Plains nations depended on the buffalo for food, clothing, shelter, and trade goods. It had religious significance for them too. But the enormous herds inter-fered directly and indirectly with the goals of US expansion. First, they sustained the Native people who resisted settler encroachment and government efforts to move them onto reservations. The buffalo also directly affected the railroads by getting in the way of construction crews and stopping trains by wandering in large numbers across the tracks. Rail travel had become essential to the goal of rapidly settling the country from coast to coast, and buffalo were in the way.

The US government set out to completely destroy the buffalo herds and force Indigenous peoples onto

DID YOU KNOW?

The animals shown in this photo are known by many different names. The Lakota people call them tatanka. The Muscogee call them yvnvsv. In the Tewa language spoken by some of the Pueblo Indians, they are kǫ?. Scientists around the world use "bison," which is rooted in Latin, and most people call them buffalo.

reservations. In May 1868 General Sherman wrote to General Sheridan, suggesting they invite sportsmen to go on a "Grand Buffalo hunt" and get rid of all of them. Under his leadership, the army sponsored and outfitted civilian hunting expeditions. Soldiers and paid hunters slaughtered tens of millions of buffalo within a few decades. Commercial hunters wanted only the skins, and so they left the rest of the animal to rot. A Kiowa woman described what the mass slaughter of the buffalo herds meant to her people:

> Everything the Kiowas had came from the buffalo. . . . Most of all, the buffalo was part of the Kiowa religion. A white buffalo calf must be sacrificed in the Sun Dance. The priests used parts of the buffalo to make their prayers when they healed people or when they sang to the powers above.
>
> . . . .
>
> Then the white men hired hunters to do nothing but kill the buffalo. Up and down the plains those men ranged, shooting sometimes as many as a hundred buffalo a day. Behind them came the skinners with their wagons. They piled the hides and bones into the wagons until they were full, and then took their loads to the new railroad stations that were being built, to be shipped east to the market. Sometimes there would be a pile of bones as high as a man, stretching a mile along the railroad track.[1]

Only a few hundred buffalo were left by the 1880s. In an effort to defend their homelands, the Sioux, Cheyenne, and Arapaho Nations formed an alliance. In

It is no accident that the buffalo were nearly extinct by the 1880s. This photograph of a man standing on the ground, with another on top of a huge pile of buffalo skulls, demonstrates the magnitude of the wanton killing of the animals during this time. Similar photos can be found, taken in other places during the same period.

1866 they killed more than eighty troops led by William Fetterman. Incidents such as the "Fetterman Fight" caused concern in Washington, DC. In 1867 President Andrew Johnson's administration sent representatives to negotiate peace treaties with leaders of dozens of Indigenous nations. Some signed on to treaties, but others refused to do so and continued their resistance to US expansion.

In 1871 Congress passed legislation that ended the authority of the president and the Senate to negotiate treaties. Congress still recognized any treaty rights that had already been negotiated, but after that, treaties and agreements between the US and Native nations would be governed by acts of Congress.

When gold rush prospectors began to flood onto Indigenous lands in California in the 1850s, conflict

APACHES AND THE US MILITARY:
THE LONGEST WAR

The Apache people resisted domination by Spain, then Mexico, long before the US annexed their territory in 1848. Warfare against the Apaches turned into the longest military engagement in US history. By 1877 the US Army had forced most Apaches onto desert reservations. Goyathlay, also called Geronimo, and his Chiricahua Apache followers refused to be confined there and evaded US forces for many years. When Geronimo finally surrendered in September of 1886 the group numbered only thirty-eight, most of them women and children. Geronimo himself was never captured.

He negotiated an agreement so that he and his band would surrender as prisoners of war. Their POW status validated Apache sovereignty and meant they could not be executed by civil authorities. On April 3, 1887, the army transported him and three hundred other Chiricahuas by train to St. Augustine, Florida, where Fort Marion was being used as a prisoner-of-war camp. Hundreds of captive Plains Indian fighters were already there. Geronimo and his people were eventually transferred to the army base at Fort Sill in Indian Territory, where they remained for the rest of their lives.

This portrait of Goyathlay, also known as Geronimo, was taken some time after his surrender, following years of conflict with the US.

was inevitable. In 1851 California's governor declared that a "war of extinction" would be waged against the Native people there. In 1864 the Modoc, Klamath, and Yahooskin Band of Snake tribes signed a treaty that ceded their lands and placed all of them in Oregon on Klamath homelands. Because the Klamath and Modocs were traditional enemies, the Modocs were not treated well on Klamath homelands. Strained relationships were made worse when government provisions promised in the treaty did not arrive. Eventually a group of Modoc families decided to return to their traditional homes in California. Their leader was Kintpuash, also known as Captain Jack.

The government sent US troops, commanded by General Edward R. S. Canby, and Oregon militiamen to capture the Modocs and take them back to Oregon. The Modocs took refuge in the barren, rugged lava beds around Lassen Peak and were able to fend off the troops for several months. Plans were made for negotiations between the soldiers and the Modocs, most of whom wanted their own reservation on their homelands in California. In a meeting on April 11, 1873, Modoc leaders killed Canby and other officials.

In response, the United States sent more than a thousand additional soldiers. By the time the Modocs were captured on June 1, 1873, the fighting had taken the lives of more than four hundred soldiers and cost the United States almost $500,000—equal to nearly $10 million today. On June 7 US Attorney General George Henry Williams advised President Grant that a military commission be appointed to decide what to do with the prisoners who had killed General Canby at what was supposed to be a diplomatic meeting. Williams's official opinion was that

> all the laws and customs of civilized warfare may not be applicable to an armed conflict with the Indian tribes upon our western frontier; but the circumstances attending the assassination of Canby [army general] and Thomas [US peace commissioner] are such as to make their murder as much a violation of the laws of savage as of civilized warfare, and the Indians concerned in it fully understood the baseness and treachery of their act.[2]

On June 8 Oregon Volunteers attacked and killed some Modoc captives who were being taken to military headquarters at Tule Lake. News of that attack inflamed public opinion. Some newspapers covering the Modoc War noted that both sides had committed murder that was beyond the expectations of "civilized warfare" and yet, soldiers, militiamen, and settler vigilantes were not being put on trial. On July 5 Kintpuash and five other Modoc men went before a military commission to face charges of murder. They were found guilty and executed by hanging on October 3, 1873. The captive Modoc families were sent to reservations.

The Fort Laramie Treaty of 1868 recognized that the Great Sioux Reservation in the Dakota Territory included the Black Hills, which are sacred to the Dakota, Lakota, and Cheyenne people. In 1874 Lieutenant Colonel George Armstrong Custer led an expedition into those sacred Black Hills. It included scientists, who confirmed that rumors of gold deposits there were true. By 1875, in violation of the Fort Laramie Treaty, the reservation was flooded with fortune seekers. This further angered tribal leaders who had signed the treaty, and the leaders of the "nontreaty" bands who had refused to sign that treaty and move onto the reservation. Congress appointed a commission to negotiate with what they called the "haughty, self important, and avaricious savages" for a way to legally open the Black Hills for Americans.[3] The negotiations were not successful, and ownership of the Black Hills remains unsettled to this day.

In June 1876 a large encampment of nontreaty Sioux and Cheyenne families was gathered along the Little Bighorn River. Later that month Custer and the Seventh Cavalry prepared to attack the encampment, but warriors led by Crazy Horse and Sitting Bull successfully intercepted them. Most textbooks call this the Battle of the Little Bighorn, but Lakota and Cheyenne people, especially those whose ancestors defended the encampment villages, know it as the Battle of the Greasy Grass. Although Custer led 225 soldiers and himself to their deaths, he was promoted to general posthumously.

HOW NEWSPAPERS SHAPED WHAT WHITE PEOPLE KNEW ABOUT INDIGENOUS PEOPLES

Many people east of the Mississippi got much of their information about the Indian Wars from the newspapers. Some articles depicted Indigenous people as brutal killers, while others reflected an understanding of their resistance.

Editorials in eastern newspapers were especially favorable toward the Nimi'ipuu (Nez Perce) leader Chief Joseph. In 1877, rather than report to a reservation, Chief

(continues on next page)

Joseph led eight hundred Nimi'ipuu civilians across Idaho Territory to get to Canada. They were pursued by two thousand soldiers of the US Cavalry. They covered about seventeen hundred miles in nearly four months while evading the soldiers and fighting hit-and-run battles.

In November 1877 the *New York Times* ran a front-page story about Chief Joseph. The writer expressed admiration for Joseph, calling his resistance "one of the most gallant and stubborn fights in the history of the Indian wars."[4] Eventually the Nimi'ipuu secured a small reservation on their Idaho homeland.

In 1878, newspaper reporters covered another dramatic pursuit when over three hundred Cheyenne left a reservation in Indian Territory. Led by resistance leaders Little Wolf and Dull Knife, they made their way toward their original homeland in what is today Wyoming and Montana. The Cheyenne were eventually intercepted by the military, but the news stories had aroused so much sympathy for them in eastern cities that the government created a reservation in a part of their original homeland.

In contrast to its coverage of the Cheyenne and Chief Joseph, the *New York Times* vilified Sitting Bull and Geronimo and their followers.

Chief Joseph received some favorable coverage in many newspapers of his day, even while evading the US Army with eight hundred of his people.

Disarmed and confined to reservations, many Indigenous peoples of the West turned to another form of resistance. The Ghost Dance, based on the prophecy of a Paiute man named Wovoka, began in Walker Lake, Nevada, and spread to other reservations. By the late 1880s Native people across the West were traveling to hear Wovoka's message and to learn the dance. Ghost Dancing, according to Wovoka's prophecy, would restore the Indigenous world as it was before colonialism, making the invaders disappear and the buffalo return. Because its purpose was to rid their homelands of Europeans, US officials saw it as a political threat.

When the dancing began on the Lakota reservations in 1890, reservation officials were afraid. On November 15 the agent at Pine Ridge sent a telegram to Washington requesting immediate protection. On November 20 the Indian Bureau in Washington drew up a list of "fomenters of disturbance" among the Ghost Dancers. Sitting Bull's name was on that list. Mindful of his role in Custer's defeat at Little Bighorn, military commanders ordered his arrest. Sitting Bull was taken into custody and held in his home, closely guarded by Indian police. On December 15, 1890, one of his captors killed him.

After Sitting Bull's death, military officials issued arrest warrants for other Indigenous leaders. When Big Foot heard the army was looking for him, he decided to lead his group of 350 men, women, and children to the Pine Ridge reservation to surrender. On the way, they encountered US troops who took them to the army camp at Wounded Knee Creek. During the night, Colonel James Forsyth and the Seventh Cavalry, Custer's old regiment, arrived. These soldiers had not forgotten that relatives of these starving, unarmed refugees had killed Custer and his troops. They aimed four Hotchkiss machine guns at the camp. The following morning, December 29, 1890, the soldiers brought the captive men out from their tipis and tents and called for all weapons to be turned in. One young man did not want to part with his Winchester rifle and, when the soldiers grabbed him, the rifle fired a shot into the air. Soldiers opened fire with rifles and the Hotchkiss guns. When the shooting ended, the troops had killed almost three hundred Sioux, including Big Foot, and twenty-five of their fellow soldiers.

ALLOTMENT

By the late 1800s the US government had forced much of the surviving Indigenous population onto small reservations, some in or near their homelands and others in Indian Territory in what is currently Oklahoma. Many Americans, however, wanted reservations broken up so the land could be available for settlers. They developed a policy of assimilation that became the General Allotment Act of 1887, known as the Dawes Act for its author, Senator Henry Dawes. Its purpose was to destroy the communal value system of Indigenous nations by turning reservations into 160-acre parcels owned by individual tribal members.

Unallotted lands were declared "surplus" and sold to settlers. In 1889 the so-called surplus land in Indian Territory was opened to settler homesteading, triggering the Oklahoma Land Run.

The Dawes Act, however, could not be applied to the five Indigenous nations that had been removed from the South, because their territories were not technically reservations: they were lands held by sovereign nations. When oil was discovered there in 1897, Congress moved to take their lands too.

The Curtis Act of 1898 amended the Dawes Act, overturning the removal treaties and dissolving the governments of the Five Civilized Tribes. The Curtis Act also required that their tribal lands be broken up and distributed to tribal members. As before, the territory left over was declared surplus and opened to homesteading. By 1907 settlers outnumbered Indigenous people in Indian Territory. Indian Territory was then dissolved and the state of Oklahoma entered the Union.

Under the Dawes and Curtis Acts, Native nations lost three-fourths of the land base that they had held after decades of army attacks and wanton land grabs. These policies had a tremendously destructive social and economic impact on Indigenous communities. Allotment ended in 1934, but the land taken was never restored and Indigenous

TO DO

Many Indigenous nations resisted the division of their lands. Sometimes resistance took the form of direct action, such as traditionalists leaving the community to live elsewhere. At other times the people took their concerns to the courts. Look into the following for a more complete picture of how Indigenous peoples resisted:

- Redbird Smith and the Cherokee opposition to allotment
- Chitto Harjo (Crazy Snake) and Muscogee resistance
- The Hopi Nation's letter to Congress, 1894

INDIAN LAND FOR SALE

GET A HOME
OF
YOUR OWN
✻
EASY PAYMENTS

PERFECT TITLE
✻
POSSESSION
WITHIN
THIRTY DAYS

FINE LANDS IN THE WEST

IRRIGATED IRRIGABLE	GRAZING	AGRICULTURAL DRY FARMING

IN 1910 THE DEPARTMENT OF THE INTERIOR SOLD UNDER SEALED BIDS ALLOTTED INDIAN LAND AS FOLLOWS:

Location.	Acres.	Average Price per Acre.	Location.	Acres.	Average Price per Acre.
Colorado	5,211.21	$7.27	Oklahoma	34,664.00	$19.14
Idaho	17,013.00	24.85	Oregon	1,020.00	15.43
Kansas	1,684.50	33.45	South Dakota	120,445.00	16.53
Montana	11,034.00	9.86	Washington	4,879.00	41.37
Nebraska	5,641.00	36.65	Wisconsin	1,069.00	17.00
North Dakota	22,610.70	9.93	Wyoming	865.00	20.64

FOR THE YEAR 1911 IT IS ESTIMATED THAT 350,000 ACRES WILL BE OFFERED FOR SALE

For information as to the character of the land write for booklet, "INDIAN LANDS FOR SALE," to the Superintendent U. S. Indian School at any one of the following places:

CALIFORNIA:	MINNESOTA:	NORTH DAKOTA:	OKLAHOMA—Con.	SOUTH DAKOTA:	WASHINGTON:
Hoopa.	Onigum.	Fort Totten.	Sac and Fox Agency.	Cheyenne Agency.	Fort Simcoe.
COLORADO:		Fort Yates.	Shawnee.	Crow Creek.	Fort Spokane.
Ignacio.	MONTANA:	OKLAHOMA:	Wyandotte.	Greenwood.	Tahoa.
IDAHO:	Crow Agency.	Anadarko.	OREGON:	Lower Brule.	Tulalip.
Lapwai.	NEBRASKA:	Cantonment.	Klamath Agency.	Pine Ridge.	WISCONSIN:
KANSAS:	Macy.	Colony.	Pendleton.	Rosebud.	Oneida.
Horton.	Santee.	Darlington.	Roseburg.	Sisseton.	
Nadeau.	Winnebago.	Muskogee.	Siletz.		
		Pawnee.			

WALTER L. FISHER,
Secretary of the Interior.

ROBERT G. VALENTINE,
Commissioner of Indian Affairs.

This poster advertises the sale of "Indian Land" by the US Department of the Interior in 1911. These "fine lands" were being made available to bidders in fourteen states. Money from the sale of the land would go to the US government, not the Native nations from which it had been taken.

peoples were never compensated for their losses.

Allotment was just one example of efforts to put an end to Indigenous nations. As you will see in the next chapter, another government program of assimilation would emerge. The Indian boarding school system took generations of children away from their families and communities and attempted to "kill the Indian" in them to make them into "civilized" Americans.[5]

The long centuries of armed conflict in defense of the homelands ended. However, through innovation and persistence Indigenous people have continued to fight to protect and preserve their lands, their languages, and their ways of life.

CHAPTER NINE

THE PERSISTENCE
OF SOVEREIGNTY

By taking over Indigenous homelands and settling from ocean to ocean, the US had fulfilled a major part of its founders' dreams. The "closing" of the American frontier seemed to create a new challenge for the United States. In your history classes, you may have heard of historian Frederick Jackson Turner and his idea that democratic civilization was a product of the settlers' experience with the American frontier. With the long era of settler colonialism and conquest ended, what would the nation be, going forward?

The so-called Turner thesis, which he first presented in 1893, became the most influential perspective on the history of the US West in the twentieth century. Turner's ideas support the popular belief in American exceptionalism, and they continue to affect how US history is taught.

However, several twenty-first-century historians see Turner's ideas as based on biases about Indigenous peoples. He believed, wrongly, that Indigenous North American cultures had no real influence on the settlers except as roadblocks to progress. He viewed Native cultures as backward and primitive in comparison with the settlers' culture, which he saw as dynamic and sophisticated. He also held the mistaken idea that the homelands of the Native people were a wilderness that had to be tamed and properly developed by settlers so that America's democracy could proceed.

Even as the United States involved itself in conflicts around the world in the latter half of the 1800s, it remained determined to acquire every last acre of Indigenous land within its borders. By the late 1800s, policies such as allotment had drastically reduced the remaining Indigenous land base. Still, Indigenous nations had homelands and reservations where they continued their traditional ways. The existence of a people with a prior claim to the land whose values, languages, and lifeways differed from those of European American society was a constant source of anxiety to white settlers. For the most part, even the settlers who opposed killing Native people outright believed in white supremacy and were profoundly uncomfortable with Native existence and sovereignty. Settler anxiety around what "ought to be done" about Native peoples was called "the Indian problem." This way of thinking about Indigenous peoples was part of Turner's error-ridden thesis. To take care of this "problem," additional policies and laws were developed. Many of those policies were based on what US officials referred to as a *choice* for Indigenous peoples: assimilate (stop being Indigenous), or become extinct. Either way, the goal was still to extinguish Indigenous nations so all their lands and resources would then be available to settlers.

In this chapter, we will first look at the Indian boarding schools, one of the earlier government-funded efforts to "do something" about Indigenous peoples by teaching them how to become more like the settlers. Then we will look at how the United States acquired what would become its forty-ninth and fiftieth states. Acquiring Alaska and Hawai'i without consent of Indigenous peoples there demonstrated that the United States' interest in expansion did not stop at its coastlines. And, as we will see later in this chapter, the US government did not hesitate to pass aggressive laws, going so far as to use the word *termina tion* to describe its goals for Indigenous peoples and their nations.

EDUCATION FOR EXTINCTION?

For decades government officials had pondered what sort of education Native children should have. In 1819 Congress passed the Indian Civilization Act, which provided thousands of dollars for missionaries to "civilize" and "Christianize" Native children at mission schools. Discussions about the role of Indian education and schools were part of treaty negotiations as Native nations ended their armed resistance and went to reservations.

During President Grant's administration, Congress budgeted $100,000 for boarding schools to be located hundreds of miles away from reservations. This move reflected the belief that the only way to educate Indigenous children to be part of settler society was to isolate them from their cultures, families, and communities. The boarding schools were modeled on treatment of Native prisoners held at Fort Marion.

In chapter 8 you read that Fort Marion, in Florida, was used as a prisoner-of-war camp from 1875 to 1878.

Captain Richard Henry Pratt was in charge of the captive Plains warriors there. On Pratt's orders, prison staff cut their hair, dressed them in army uniforms, had them drill like soldiers, and assigned them to manual labor such as picking fruit. Pratt considered this such a success that he followed the same model when he established the Carlisle Indian Industrial School in Pennsylvania in 1879.

Similar boarding schools also used the word *industrial* or *training* in their names to signify that the program emphasized skills students would need for various types of manual labor. The industrial school model began in the 1800s in England, where boarding schools were created to train juvenile delinquents and children from families living in poverty.

The photos below show Indigenous students in classes at the Carlisle Indian Industrial School. The boys (left photo) are learning how to work with metal. The school assumed that Native girls would know nothing about domestic arts (cooking, cleaning, sewing, and so on) and required them to attend classes where they could "learn" how to do things like iron clothes (right photo).

Supported by Congress, Carlisle was the prototype for the other federal boarding schools set up across the

continent soon after. When Alaska became a US territory, churches and the government set up similar schools there. Indigenous children were taken from their homes—sometimes with their parents' consent, sometimes by force. School officials cut their hair, changed their names, replaced their traditional clothing with uniforms, and had them sleep in barracks-like dormitories. Boarding school education included typical subjects, in addition to marching in formation and preparing for jobs as farmhands, carpenters, or domestic servants.

Some parents chose to send their children to the schools. The government's violations of treaty agreements brought hardships that made it almost impossible for parents to properly care for their children. In some instances, parents believed their children would, at least, be fed at a boarding school. Others hoped that their children would learn English and be able to use

In order to "prove" the schools were successfully assimilating Native children into white society, "before and after" photos of them were taken and used to solicit funding for the schools. The "before" photos showed them in their traditional clothing, as if that clothing proved they had been "savage." The "after" photos, like this one, suggested that they had become "civilized."

the education they received to help fight ongoing treaty violations and exploitation by merchants, settlers, and government agents.

In 1939 the philanthropist Edwin Embree published an account of a visit he had with a man he called Sun Elk, who was thought to have been the first child from

WHO WAS SUN ELK?

The source for the Sun Elk quote is Edwin R. Embree's book *Indians of the Americas: Historical Pageant.* That quote is found in many books and articles about the Carlisle Indian Industrial School, but there are no records of a person with that name being there. Carlisle does have records for a person named Lorenzo Martinez who was from Taos and went to Carlisle at roughly the same time (1884 to 1889). You can see his records, like the post-card shown here, online by going to the website for the Carlisle Indian School Digital Resource Center and entering his name into the search box.

Comparisons between what Embree provided and other writings about Lorenzo Martinez strongly suggest that "Sun Elk" and Lorenzo Martinez are the same person. Other books and reports refer to Lorenzo Martinez and say that he was at Carlisle.

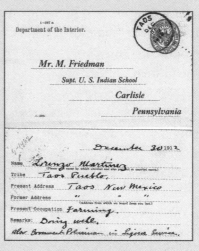

In 1906 Lorenzo Martinez was the interpreter for Matilda Coxe Stephenson, an anthropologist who wanted to study Taos culture. In 1920 he went to Washington, DC, to serve as the interpreter when the governor of Taos, Porfirio Mirabel, was meeting with members of Congress about land disputes.

Some of the language Embree attributes to Sun Elk does not seem quite right. Sun Elk, for example, uses "priest and delight makers" to describe religious figures. We wonder if Embree sub-stituted those words for the ones that Sun Elk/Lorenzo Martinez actually used. And we wonder if "Sun Elk" is a name that Embree created or if Lorenzo Martinez used that name as well. It is also possible that "Sun Elk" is a stage name that Martinez used with tourists he encountered while in Taos or while traveling elsewhere.

There are many examples of a Native person's speech being modified by a writer. One example is a picture book titled *Brother Eagle, Sister Sky*. The author is listed as Chief Seattle, but the words in that book are not what Sealth (the name he actually used) said. They are closer to what a screenwriter named Ted Perry created in 1971 for *Home*, a television show about ecology.

We pose the question "Who Was Sun Elk?" to encourage you to question what you find in books that attribute remarks to a Native person.

Taos Pueblo to attend Carlisle beginning in 1883. Embree quoted Sun Elk's comments about his years at Carlisle.

> They told us that Indian ways were bad. They said we must get civilized. I remember that word too. It means "be like the white man." I am willing to be like the white man, but I did not believe Indians' ways were wrong. But they kept teaching us for seven years. And the books told how bad the Indians had been to the white men—burning their towns and killing their women and children. But I had seen white men do that to Indians. We all wore white man's clothes and ate white man's food and went to white man's churches and spoke white man's talk. And so after a while we also began to say Indians were bad. We laughed at our own people and their blankets and cooking pots and sacred societies and Dances.[1]

Physical punishment was not typical in Indigenous families but was routine in the boarding schools. The children were made to feel that it was criminal to be Indian. They could be beaten or physically punished for such things as speaking their own languages and practicing their cultural traditions. Many students who experienced such harsh treatment were psychologically damaged. Today we might say that they had post-traumatic stress disorder (PTSD). Even when they were done with boarding school, they carried the hurt with them into adulthood, and it often surfaced in their interactions with their families and communities. One woman talked about the long-term effects of her mother's boarding school experience:

> And the stories she told . . . were horrendous. There were beatings . . . and having to kneel for hours on cold basement floors as punishment. . . . My mother lived with a rage all her life, and I think the fact that they were taken away so young was part of this rage and how it—the fallout—was on us as a family.[2]

When the effects of an experience like this are passed on to one's children in this way, it is called *intergenerational trauma*.

Sexual abuse of both girls and boys in the missionary and boarding schools was rampant. As sometimes happens today, adults in positions of authority sexually harassed, exploited, and abused young people in their care. The children were too far from home to turn to their parents for protection. Even at those times when they could tell their parents what happened, the parents, many of whom had been sexually abused at the schools too, might not have known how to help them.

Indigenous children at the schools often ran away to escape the physical, emotional, and sexual abuse they endured. In some instances, they died trying to get home.

Indigenous parents and their children found ways to resist the boarding schools' agenda and the harmful practices students encountered there. Running away from school was the most common way Indigenous children resisted. There were also acts of sabotage and refusal to participate. Many children continued to speak their languages and practice their ceremonies in secret. This resilience helps to explain why so many survived. Even so, the damage to so many children, families, and communities was lasting and is hard to fully understand.

■ BEYOND "FROM SEA TO SHINING SEA"

At the same time that the United States was brutally colonizing, relocating, and killing Indigenous peoples of the Americas, it was using similar methods to pursue overseas dominance. Between 1798 and 1919 the US military intervened and in some cases occupied nations on every continent except Antarctica. Through these interventions it added to its territories and eventually added what would become its forty-ninth and fiftieth states in 1959.

For thousands of years, the Kanaka Maoli (native Hawaiians) lived on the islands that are currently known as Hawai'i. The people of different islands shared a common language and respect for the land as something to embrace rather than exploit. Hawaiians supported their communities by farming and fishing. By 1810 the islands were united under the mo'i (highest ruler) Kamehameha. Although the Hawaiian social and political structure was stratified, relationships among the classes were closer and relatively respectful compared to the oppressiveness of the

The Hawaiian people have been publishing newspapers in their language since the mid-1800s. This image shows the front page of *Ko Hawaii Pae Aina*, a Hawaiian-language newspaper published in Honolulu in 1878.

European system of royalty, nobility, and commoners discussed in the beginning of this book. Just as they had with Indigenous peoples of the Americas, Europeans generally viewed native Hawaiians as exotic, primitive heathens. Calvinist missionaries from the United States began arriving around 1820, and French priests of the Catholic Church arrived in the 1830s.

Many Kanaka Maoli recognized that they were vulnerable to colonization by Europe and the United States. They made a strategic decision to use the Europeans' tools such as writing and treaty making to secure their national sovereignty. The US recognized Hawaiian independence in 1826. In 1840 the Kanaka Maoli created a constitution and made laws in much the same ways that the British and US governments did. In 1843 Great Britain and France signed a joint proclamation recognizing Hawai'i as an independent nation. Eventually Hawaiians began electing their mo'i.

A series of treaties enabled the United States to expand its whaling industry into Hawaiian waters and to use Hawaiian agricultural land for sugar plantations. By the mid-1880s, haole (non-Hawaiians) had gained significant influence. In 1887 a group of haole men (sons and grandsons of the Calvinist missionaries and planters) with the support of the US military were able to force the mo'i to approve a constitution that surrendered most of their political power. The Hawaiian people used diplomatic and other nonviolent means to resist this US interference with their sovereignty. But in 1893, with US support, a group of powerful haoles overthrew the moʻi Liliuokalani, imprisoned her, and installed a haole president. Despite diplomatic and other nonviolent resistance by many Kanaka Maoli, the US annexed Hawaii in 1898.

Liliuokalani published her memoir, *Hawaii's Story by Hawaii's Queen*, In 1898, the same year the US annexed Hawaii. It includes this portrait of her.

For thousands of years, the homelands of the Indigenous people of what is currently known as the state of Alaska have included coastal regions, temperate rainforest, and Arctic tundra. Their population consists of hundreds of distinct groups speaking more than twenty different languages. The word "Alaska" is derived from an Unangan word that means "place the sea moves toward."[3]

Colonizer contact with Indigenous peoples began around 1741 when a Russian mapping expedition led by Vitus Bering reached the area. A number of commercial

DID YOU KNOW?

The term "Unangan" may be unfamiliar to you, but it is the preferred term of the people who are commonly known as the Aleuts. Some view "Aleut" and other common terms, such as "Eskimo," in a negative way; they are words the colonizers used, not the people themselves. We encourage you to use a people's preferred terms for themselves.

expeditions followed, focused mainly on finding fur-bearing animals. Sea otter pelts were especially sought after. They were as valuable at that time as oil is today. The first Russian settlement was established in 1784. The Indigenous people fought to protect their communities and resources from the Russians but were overwhelmed by Russia's weaponry. During the "fur rush," Russians forced Indigenous men to do the hunting by threatening to kill their families if they did not bring back enough furs. Russian colonization of Alaska lasted less than a century. In that time the sea otter population was hunted to near extinction.

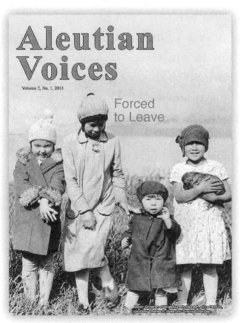

During World War II, the US government forcibly removed Indigenous Alaskans from their homes on islands strategically important to the US military. In more recent times, films, books, and magazines like *Aleutian Voices* have shed light on that traumatic period.

Russia's desire to control Alaska faded as the fur trade declined and the Russian empire expanded elsewhere. In 1867 Russia sold six-hundred-thousand square miles of Alaska to the United States for $7.2 million, and the US began its exploitation of Alaska's other resources. A series of gold rushes began in 1880. Mining destroyed streams, forests, and other ecosystems in the Native Alaska homelands. Game animals and other wildlife central to the Indigenous peoples' lives lost much of their habitat, and the people suffered from a variety of diseases brought by the miners. Alaska also became the world's largest producer of canned salmon, but the canneries were owned by settlers, and Native rights to fish were restricted.

White missionaries and settlers in Alaska spoke of Native people as savage and inferior. Racial discrimination and segregation were legal. Indigenous peoples could be excluded from businesses and public places, and their children could not attend public schools with whites. In the early 1900s a group of Indigenous Alaskans formed the Alaska Native Brotherhood (ANB) and the Alaska Native Sisterhood (ANS) to resist segregation, forced assimilation, and efforts to take their lands. Their work led to several landmarks in social justice. They secured voting rights for Native Alaskans in 1922, and in 1945 they moved the Alaska territorial legislature to pass the Alaska Civil Rights Act. Successful protests by the ANB and ANS predate those in the United States by several years, and it is recognized as the oldest Native American civil rights organization in the US.

PUSHING BACK AGAINST LEGALIZED LAND THEFT

The years from 1872 to 1956 can be seen as a continuation of the US government's efforts to take land and resources from Indigenous nations. Legal agreements that described reservation boundaries and who could and could not enter there were upended again and again. Some of these reversals may have appeared benevolent in the eyes of the general public, such as the creation of national parks, but these decisions usually served to legally separate Indigenous peoples from their resources.

In 1872 Congress passed the Yellowstone Park Act, turning it into land for "public use," which meant people could visit, camp, and enjoy the natural sights in the park's boundaries. The land set aside for the park was not considered Indigenous land, but Indigenous peoples had "reserved rights," meaning they could hunt, fish, or travel on those lands. Records indicate that Shoshones, Bannocks, Crow, and others were exercising those rights.

Yellowstone was the first national park in the United States. Other "public use" areas were also created from Indigenous land, with distinctions regarding how, when, and by whom these areas could be used. As of 2018 the US Forest Service system includes 154 protected forests and 20 grasslands. The national park system now includes fifty-nine national parks and more than three hundred national monuments, seashores, lakeshores, and battlefields. In many cases the government attempted to terminate the rights of Indigenous peoples to use those lands for hunting and for ceremonies. But there is also a long history of Indigenous peoples fighting to keep or regain lands taken for public use. One example is Taos Pueblo's effort to get Blue Lake back into their control.

On November 7, 1906, President Theodore Roosevelt signed a proclamation that took Blue Lake and thousands of acres of Taos Pueblo homelands and made them part of Carson National Forest. Blue Lake is the heart of their cultural and ceremonial traditions, and the people of Taos Pueblo spent the next sixty-four years fighting to get it returned to them. During that time, the US Congress passed several laws that had significant bearing on Indigenous land claims. Eventually Taos Pueblo was able to win back Blue Lake; you will find more about that in the next chapter.

By the early 1920s the Pueblos of New Mexico had been trying for some time to get non-Indigenous settlers to leave Pueblo land. When US Senator Holm Bursum of New Mexico introduced legislation that would have given land and water rights to those non-Indigenous settlers, a delegation of Pueblo leaders went to Washington, DC, to address Congress. Their statement said, in part:

> We have never asked for this legislation. We were never given a chance of having anything to say or do about this bill. We have studied the bill over and found that this bill will deprive us of our happy life by taking away our lands and water and will destroy our Pueblo government and our customs which we have enjoyed for hundreds of years, and through which we have been able to be self-supporting and happy down to this day.[4]

The Pueblo efforts to keep their land were covered favorably in some newspapers of the day. A number of influential non-Indigenous peoples added their voices to those of the Pueblo leaders. The Bursum Bill was defeated. Congress then passed the Pueblo Lands Act in

1924. The Lands Act established the Pueblo Lands Board to investigate claims to disputed territory. Although the board tended to favor non-Native settlers, some of its decisions led to better outcomes for the Pueblos than would have been possible otherwise.

John Collier, who had been a strong advocate for the Pueblos during their land claims struggle, served as Commissioner of Indian Affairs from 1933 to 1945. In that post he worked closely with Native communities to draft the Indian Reorganization Act (IRA) of 1934. The IRA ended further allotment of Indigenous territories and committed the federal government to purchasing available land that bordered reservations in order to restore lands to relevant Native nations. The IRA also included a provision that set up a process for tribal nations to establish constitutionally representative governments if they wanted to replace existing ones. Several, including the Navajo Nation, chose to keep their traditional government. The IRA is the foundation of contemporary federal legislation in Indian affairs. It marks the first time that Congress formally recognized and actively supported the authority of tribal communities to make and be governed by their own laws.[6]

When President Harry Truman took office in 1945, Collier and other progressive appointees from President Franklin Roosevelt's New Deal were pushed out. New legislation moved away from support for Indigenous sovereignty. In 1946 Congress established the Indian Claims Court and the Indian Claims Commission. Their stated purpose was to allow Native nations to file suit to recover lands that were illegally taken or to receive some payment for the loss of those lands. The outcome, however, was similar to what happened with claims heard by the Pueblo Lands Board. Despite what they were promised, Indigenous nations were not fairly compensated for the loss of their lands. In creating the Indian Claims Commission, Congress acknowledged that the federal government had, in fact, violated treaties when it seized Indigenous lands. Indigenous nations were able to use that acknowledgment later to strengthen their sovereignty and reclaim land.

By the late 1940s Congress was trying to repeal the Indian Reorganization Act and end the relationship between the federal government and the Indian tribes. In 1953 it introduced the first of several policies that terminated the sovereign status of several tribal nations. This meant that the government would cut off federal funds to the tribe, disband its tribal government, and turn its tribally owned businesses into small businesses owned by individuals. The commissioner of Indian affairs in charge of this effort, Dillon S. Myer, commented that Indigenous consent for this drastic policy change was irrelevant: "We must proceed even though Indian cooperation may be lacking in certain cases."[7]

During the Termination Era, a number of federal policies were created that were meant to undermine Native nations. For example, Public Law 280 transferred police power on some reservations from the federal government to the states, without consent of the tribal governments.

Congress also began drafting legislation to terminate the sovereign nation status of several Native nations. The Menominee Nation of Wisconsin was the first to be terminated. On June 17, 1954, President Dwight D. Eisenhower issued a statement that suggested the Menominee people were in full support of termination. They were not. For years they would fight it and ultimately prevail in having their status as a sovereign nation restored. Between 1953 and 1966 more than one hundred tribal nations were terminated. Some are still fighting to regain federal recognition of their sovereignty, while other have succeeded in having theirs restored.

Supreme Court decisions made during the nineteenth century enabled the US to justify undermining Native sovereignty and depriving Native nations of their land base. During the Termination Era, it used those decisions in its continual push to force Native people to assimilate. One such effort was the 1956 Indian Relocation Act (Public

Law 949). Under Relocation, the Bureau of Indian Affairs (BIA) would provide funding for any Indigenous individual or family to relocate to specific urban areas, including San Francisco, Denver, and Cleveland. This project gave rise to large Native urban populations scattered among poor and working-class neighborhoods where they found low-paying jobs and faced long-term unemployment. But they also created support centers where they carried on with their community-oriented value systems and worked together to organize political actions.

■ ■ ■

The Termination and Relocation Acts of the 1950s were part of the centuries-long efforts to dispossess Indigenous peoples. The removals of the 1830s took Native people from their lands, relocating them by force and federal law, to Indian Territory. The boarding schools of the late 1800s removed children from their families and communities. The new termination policies attempted to deprive entire nations of their right to exist, and the Relocation Act was an attempt to entice entire families to abandon their homelands and their communities.

In spite of everything the United States government tried to do, Indigenous peoples refused to stop being Indigenous. Instead, they organized and worked together wherever they were to support each other and their identities. In short, they resisted. In the decade of protests in the 1960s they would organize political actions that would seize the country's attention.

CHAPTER TEN

INDIGENOUS ACTION, INDIGENOUS RIGHTS

You may have read in history classes about the political and social upheavals of the 1960s. The emphasis was probably on the civil rights of African Americans and the protests against US military involvement in Vietnam, but Indigenous peoples were politically engaged too on several fronts. Their activism can be described as a persistent, organized, and increasingly intertribal resistance to federal policies that undermined Indigenous self-determination and sovereignty.

Some of this intertribal activism had roots in organizations founded during the 1940s. One of the first international, intertribal organizations was the Inter-American Indian Institute, which was established in 1940. As part of the Organization of American States, the institute brought Indigenous peoples of the Americas together to work on issues

This tipi was erected near the Washington Monument in 1978 for the Longest Walk, one of many events during which Indigenous people have erected tipis at the National Mall.

that concerned all of them. Within the US, the National Congress of American Indians (NCAI, founded in 1944) participated in much of the Indigenous activism of the 1960s and beyond. It remains the oldest, largest, and most representative organization of American Indian and Alaska Native nations.

Native elders brought to these organizations the wisdom and experience gained in lifetimes of fighting for their rights, but new energy and direction came from a rising generation of activists. This chapter looks at some key moments of Indigenous activism from the 1960s through 2013.

FISH-INS AND OCCUPATIONS: INDIGENOUS ACTIVISM IN THE 1960S

When John F. Kennedy won the presidency in 1960, Indigenous peoples believed they had an opportunity to push hard against government programs like termination and to push for policies that would support Native sovereignty. In 1961 an intertribal group of Native people gathered at a conference in Chicago. Their goal was to finalize a document called the Declaration of Indian Purpose that would lay out a new path for Native nations. The completed Declaration emphasized Native self-determination and set out demands for the federal government that included giving greater attention to issues related to health, education, and resource development in Native communities. It was eventually presented to President Kennedy.

Among the conference attendees was a group of college students who had been meeting frequently over the previous two years to talk about the changes they felt were necessary. The tone and direction of the conference frustrated them. One student, Clyde Warrior (Ponca), later commented:

> It was sickening to see American Indians get up and tell obvious lies about how well the federal government was treating them. . . . What was happening was these tribal officials, or finks, were just going into that gear of appealing to the Great White Father again.[1]

In 1961 that group of students formed the National Indian Youth Council (NIYC). It included twenty-six young Native people from twenty-one Native nations. Their founding document expressed their commitment to what they called "a greater Indian America":

> At this time in the history of the American Indian, we, the younger generation, find it expedient to band together on a national scale in meeting the challenges facing Indian people. In banding for mutual assistance we recognize that the future of the Indian people will ultimately rest in the hands of the younger people, and that Indian youth need be concerned with the position of the American Indian. We further recognize the inherent strength of the American Indian heritage that will be enhanced by a national Indian organization. The needs of the American Indians to be served are numerous and varied. Besides needs there are contributions already made and more to be made to America by its original inhabitants. We believe in a greater Indian America.[2]

In January of 1964 the chairman of the Makah Nation asked NIYC to assist several Native nations fighting to protect treaty-guaranteed fishing rights in Washington State. Activists organized several nonviolent actions that gained media attention, including a mass demonstration in Seattle in February 1964. That action led to a meeting in March 1964 between fishing rights groups and the Washington governor. Although most of the demands they presented to the governor were not met, NIYC representative Hank Adams (Assiniboine-Sioux) later noted that they were able to propose "a very positive and constructive approach to the solution of the various problems and issues" Native people faced in the Pacific Northwest.[3] That same year, Adams and other leaders founded the Survival of American Indians Association. Composed of Swinomish, Nisqually, Yakama, Puyallup, Stillaguamish, and other Indigenous peoples of the Pacific Northwest, its

In 1966, members of the Muckleshoot Indian Tribe in the state of Washington organized a "Treaty Trek" to call attention to their fishing rights.

Puyallup tribal citizen Allison Bridges was arrested during a September 4, 1970, raid on a fishing encampment.

purpose was to carry on the battle to protect their rights to fish in their traditional fishing waters. The backlash against the fish-ins from law enforcement and from non-Native sport fishers was often violent. Local and state police smashed the Indigenous peoples' fishing boats and confiscated their gear on more than one occasion. People were sometimes seriously injured, and many were arrested during incidents over the years.

The fish-in movement lasted many years and put the tiny community at Frank's Landing in Washington State in the headlines. It was a significant moment for many Native people. Sid Mills (Yakima and Cherokee) was among the many younger people who joined the protests at Frank's Landing. After his arrest there in 1968, Mills stated that though he was a Vietnam veteran, he had no further obligation to the United States:

> My first obligation now lies with the Indian People fighting for the lawful Treaty to fish in usual and accustomed water of the Nisqually, Columbia and other rivers of the Pacific Northwest, and in serving them in this fight in any way possible. . . . We will fight for our rights.[4]

The fish-in movement was one case of local organizing and action to protect Indigenous peoples' rights.

Community-level organizing was also happening in urban areas that had large, multitribal Indigenous populations due to Relocation. In Minneapolis, for example, Indigenous peoples were frequently racially profiled and harassed by the police. Two Ojibwe men, Dennis Banks and Clyde Bellecourt, organized informal patrols to escort Native people in areas where the harassment was especially blatant. By 1968 their local organization had grown into the American Indian Movement (AIM). AIM's confrontational approach to activism began attracting members from many Native nations.

While local actions multiplied in Native communities and nations, the spectacular November 1969 seizure and occupation of Alcatraz Island in San Francisco Bay grabbed nationwide attention. Alcatraz, also known as "The Rock," was the site of a federal prison until the government closed it and abandoned the island in 1963. Like Minneapolis, the Bay Area had a substantial Native population due to the Relocation program. The Indian Friendship Center

DID YOU KNOW?

In 1973 fourteen of the fishing nations (tribal nations that rely on fishing as a primary source of food and income) sued Washington State. The following year, US District Court judge George Boldt found in their favor. He validated their right to 50 percent of fish taken "in the usual and accustomed places"[5] that were designated in the 1850s treaties, even where those places were not currently within reservation boundaries. This was a landmark decision. Indigenous nations in other parts of the country also fought for their treaty-based hunting and fishing rights. Some had significant wins in the courts. The outcome of a fishing-rights case led Wisconsin to pass Act 31, which requires that the public schools teach about the history, culture, and tribal sovereignty of Indigenous nations in Wisconsin.

there had become an important meeting place for many who were far from their home communities. They eased their feelings of isolation by creating clubs based on tribal affiliation, such as the Sioux Club and the Navajo Club. They discussed ways to make life better for Native people. A woman in the Sioux Club, Belva Cottier, read in the newspaper that the government was in the process of deciding what to do with Alcatraz. She and some relatives and friends studied the terms of the 1868 Treaty of Fort Laramie, which said abandoned federal lands would revert to tribal ownership. They understood this to mean that Alcatraz was Indigenous property.[6]

On March 8, 1964, a group that included several members of the Sioux Club dressed in powwow regalia took a boat to Alcatraz. They symbolically claimed the land for Native people by pounding stakes into the earth, as Lewis and Clark had done on their "expedition" across

Belva Cottier (Sioux), right, and a young Chicano friend on Alcatraz Island during the occupation, taken May 30, 1971. Cottier was a key organizer of the first occupation of Alcatraz in 1964.

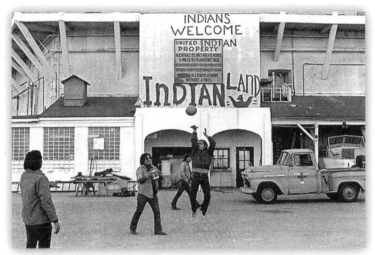

In the background of this photograph, someone has painted "Indians Welcome. United Indian Property. Indian Land" on the wall of a building on Alcatraz. On the ground below, young Native men are checking out sports equipment.

Indigenous homelands in the 1800s.[7] They did not stay long on Alcatraz, but shortly afterward, they filed a legal claim to get the island back for Native people.

That brief action and the court case paved the way for the larger occupation.

In November 1969 a group that called itself Indians of All Tribes organized another takeover of Alcatraz. They, too, used the 1868 Treaty of Fort Laramie to support their claim that abandoned federal lands would revert to tribal ownership and announced that Alcatraz was Indian land. They set up a thriving village on the island that became a focal point for Indigenous activism.

The occupation of Alcatraz drew thousands of Native people, including families, from all over the continent. Some stayed only a short time; others remained there for more than a year. Indigenous women like Madonna

Many families with children joined the occupation of Alcatraz. During the day, they did the same sort of activities that children everywhere did, like riding bikes.

Thunderhawk (Cheyenne River Sioux Tribe), LaNada Means War Jack (Shoshone), and Rayna Ramirez (Winnebago Tribe of Nebraska) held leadership positions on Alcatraz. The occupiers' "Proclamation of the Indians of All Tribes" expressed Indigenous solidarity, sarcasm, and good humor:

> We, the Native Americans, reclaim the land known as Alcatraz Island in the name of all American Indians by right of discovery.
>
> We wish to be fair and honorable in our dealings with the Caucasian inhabitants of this land, and hereby offer the following treaty:
>
> We will purchase said Alcatraz Island for twenty-four dollars (24) in glass beads and red cloth, a prece-

dent set by the white man's purchase of a similar island about 300 years ago. . . .

We will give to the inhabitants of this island a portion of the land for their own to be held in trust by the American Indians Government and by the bureau of Caucasian Affairs to hold in perpetuity—for as long as the sun shall rise and the rivers go down to the sea. We will further guide the inhabitants in the proper way of living. We will offer them our religion, our education, our life-ways, in order to help them achieve our level of civilization and thus raise them and all their white brothers up from their savage and unhappy state. . . .

Further, it would be fitting and symbolic that ships from all over the world, entering the Golden Gate, would first see Indian land, and thus be reminded of the true history of this nation. This tiny island would be a symbol of the great lands once ruled by free and noble Indians.[8]

Though some of the language in the proclamation was a clever play on colonialist language that had long

DID YOU KNOW?

The year 1964 was not the first time Indigenous peoples were on Alcatraz Island. In the late 1800s the island was a military installation. The army used it as a place to confine members of the Hopi Nation who resisted the US government's assimilation policies by refusing to send their children to boarding schools like those you read about in chapter 9.

romanticized and misrepresented Indigenous peoples, Indians of All Tribes was not playing around. They demanded that five institutions be established on Alcatraz:

- a center for Native American studies
- an American Indian spiritual center
- an Indian center of ecology that would do scientific research on reversing pollution of water and air
- a training school that would provide job training and teach "the noble and tragic events of Indian history, including the broken treaties, the documentary of the Trail of Tears, the Massacre of Wounded Knee, as well as the victory over Yellow Hair Custer and his army"[9]
- a memorial as a reminder that the island had been established as a prison initially to incarcerate and execute California Indian resisters to US assault on their nations

By the time the occupation of Alcatraz ended, it had inspired thousands of people, especially Indigenous youth, to become more politically engaged. During the eighteen-month occupation, the population on Alcatraz shifted as new people arrived and others left. But in June of 1971, under orders from President Richard Nixon's administration, the remaining Indigenous residents were forced to evacuate Alcatraz. Some of the demands for Native institutions were addressed after the occupation ended. Indigenous professors Jack Forbes and David Risling negotiated a grant of unused federal land and established Deganawidah-Quetzalcoatl University in 1971 as a two-year Native American–Chicano college. University of

California at Davis became the first US university to offer a doctorate in Native American studies.

The Indigenous organizations formed during the 1960s used a range of strategies but shared a commitment to principles that reflected basic concerns facing all Native nations: treaty rights, tribal sovereignty, self-determination, and cultural preservation. Those common principles enabled a number of Native-led groups to join forces in 1972 for another event that caught the attention of the media and the general public: the Trail of Broken Treaties.

THE LEGACY OF BROKEN TREATIES: INDIGENOUS ACTIVISM IN THE 1970S

The Trail of Broken Treaties was a cross-country intertribal caravan of Indigenous peoples, coordinated by a coalition of eight Indigenous organizations, including NIYC, AIM, and NCAI. In October 1972, carloads of Native people set out for Washington, DC, stopping at reservations and other Indigenous communities on their way. The numbers of vehicles and participants multiplied at each stop. Around eight hundred Indigenous peoples from many tribal nations arrived in Washington just before the presidential election. They planned to meet with federal officials and present a twenty-point position paper that described the government's responsibilities to Indigenous nations.

Bureau of Indian Affairs (BIA) employees had been instructed not to assist the Trail of Broken Treaties caravan in any way. When the caravan got to Washington, most of the travelers went right to the Bureau of Indian Affairs building, where they waited to learn where they would be staying. When suitable lodging proved unavailable, it was agreed that the group could stay in the auditorium of the Department of the Interior building. As they started to leave the BIA for the Department of Interior, a scuffle with security guards ended with a decision not to leave at all. When police threatened to remove them, they used furniture to barricade doors and make weapons for self-defense. The audacious occupation of the BIA got a great deal of media attention. Celebrities and key figures in the civil rights movement, such as Dr. Benjamin Spock and Stokely Carmichael, offered their support.

Native people occupying the Bureau of Indian Affairs building drew media attention by actions such as hanging a banner declaring that the building was now the "Native American Embassy."

The occupation lasted six days. It ended with promises that charges would not be filed against any of the occupiers and with an agreement that the Nixon administration would review and respond to the "Twenty Points" paper within sixty days.

The government's response to the Twenty Points was profoundly disappointing. Native people around the country were angered by the government's apparent unwillingness to engage with their deepest concerns.

Three months after the BIA building takeover, some Oglala Lakota people at the

Pine Ridge Sioux Reservation in western South Dakota invited the American Indian Movement to assist them with ongoing conflict there. They were concerned about the threatening and sometimes violent actions of Tribal Chairman Richard Wilson, the tribal police, and Wilson's private security force, called Guardians of the Oglala Nation (also called the GOONs). Local people met with AIM leaders, including Pine Ridge citizen Russell Means, on February 27, 1973. The meeting ended with a decision to lead a caravan to the tiny town of Wounded Knee to protest the chairman's misdeeds and the violence of his GOONs. It was soon apparent that law enforcement was anticipating violent confrontation. The Federal Bureau of Investigation, tribal police, and the GOONs followed the caravan. Over the following days hundreds more armed men surrounded Wounded Knee, along with Huey helicopters and military snipers. It was the beginning of a two-and-a-half-month siege of Indigenous peoples at the same place where the mass slaughter of Big Foot and his people took place in 1890.

Law enforcement exchanged thousands of rounds of gunfire with the Indigenous peoples who gathered at Wounded Knee. By the time the siege ended in May, the only structure of the village that was not damaged was the mass grave in which Big Foot and his people were buried. Two Native men were killed by gunfire and a federal marshal was seriously injured. The government spent millions of dollars to contain the Wounded Knee protest, but it could not control one of the most significant outcomes of the long standoff: a renewed sense of accomplishment and unity among Native people across the United States.

This woodcut poster was created in 1970 by non-Native artist Bruce Carter as part of his Wounded Knee series about the 1890 massacre. It was used in the newspaper *Akwesasne Notes* three years later to mark the connection between that massacre and the 1973 events at Wounded Knee.

Native activism in the 1970s was not limited to demonstrations, caravans, and occupations. Indigenous peoples' determined fight to keep their sovereignty and their nations intact took them to courtrooms and to the halls of Congress, where they pressed for the demise of termination policies and the passage of several important laws. The Indian Self-Determination and Education Assistance Act, passed in 1975, acknowledged that tribal nations had the authority to determine their needs and decide how they would use federal money to meet those needs. The law gave many Native nations the impetus to develop strong political systems and community services, including health care, education support, economic development programs, and police and fire protection for their citizens.

Another key federal law grounded in Native self-determination and sovereignty is the Indian Child Welfare Act (ICWA) of 1978. Before ICWA, between 25 and 35 percent of all Native children had been removed from their homes and communities by state and county social service agencies. This was often done with the help of courts that showed clear preference for placing the children with non-Native families. The agencies and the courts also showed a pattern of making little effort to support Native families who qualified for their services or to help them get their children back. At the conclusion of a years-long congressional investigation, Senator James Abourezk, the chairman of the Subcommittee on Indian Affairs, said:

> Welfare workers and social workers who are handling child welfare caseloads use any means available, whether legal or illegal, coercive or cajoling or whatever, to get the children away from mothers they think are not fit. In many cases they were lied to, they were given documents to sign and they were deceived about the contents of the documents.[10]

The outcome of the congressional investigation was ICWA. Section 3 of the act says that the purpose of ICWA is to

> protect the best interests of Indian children and to promote the stability and security of Indian tribes and families by the establishment of minimum Federal standards for the removal of Indian children from their families and the placement of such children in foster or adoptive homes which will reflect the unique values of Indian culture, and by providing for assistance to Indian tribes in the operation of child and family service programs.

The phrase "stability and security" recognizes that for tribal nations to continue to exist as sovereign entities, they need their children to remain as tribal citizens. "The best interests of Indian children" means that Native

In 2016 mainstream media covered the court removal of a Choctaw child from her foster placement with a white family. The media failed to inform readers and listeners about the purpose of and the need for the Indian Child Welfare Act. When news media are reporting on ICWA cases, we recommend you read and listen to Native media who can accurately report on cases like that. Two good places to start are the websites of the Native American Rights Fund (NARF) and the National Indian Child Welfare Association (NICWA).

children in the child protection or welfare system are to be placed with Native relatives or within their Native communities if at all possible, so they do not lose their connections to their Native nation, families, and communities.

The process of determining where a Native child will be placed is more complicated than it may seem, and it is clear from some recent court cases that got media attention that some agencies still do not follow ICWA protocols as they should.

The activism of the 1960s and 1970s brought greater public attention to Native sovereignty and other concerns of Indigenous nations in the United States. At the same time, Indigenous peoples around the globe were making their voices heard in their homelands.

INDIGENOUS ACTIVISM ON A GLOBAL STAGE

During the 1970s Indigenous peoples in the US began to seek "the recognition by the nations of the world of their rightful status as nations in the community of nations," according to Standing Rock Sioux scholar Vine Deloria Jr.[11]

Less than a year after the 1973 standoff at Wounded Knee, more than five thousand Indigenous people, including representatives from Latin America and Pacific Island nations, met and founded the International Indian Treaty Council (IITC). The IITC then organized the first conference to be held at the United Nations on Indigenous Peoples of the Americas in 1977. This conference was an important step toward international recognition that Indigenous peoples around the globe all faced similar challenges related to their history of colonization and exploitation by European countries. A sense of solidarity grew among the Indigenous peoples there. The "Twenty Points" framework that had gone to Washington, DC, with the Trail of Broken Treaties was shared at the conference. It eventually became the basis for the United Nations Declaration on the Rights of Indigenous Peoples.

In 1987 the United Nations appointed a special investigator to assess treaties and agreements Indigenous nations entered into with other nations, including ones made with the original colonizers (such as France or England) and with the national governments that emerged later, such as the United States and Australia. The findings of the investigation were issued in a final report published

DID YOU KNOW?

Vine Deloria Jr. is credited by many scholars as being one of the founders of Indigenous studies. His book *Custer Died for Your Sins*, for example, was read by many of the young people who were at Alcatraz. We recommend you get to know his work, which is known for its humor as well as its insight into the relationships between Indigenous peoples and the United States.

DID YOU KNOW?

The UN General Assembly passed the Declaration on the Rights of Indigenous Peoples in 2007. The Declaration states that Indigenous peoples have

> the right to the full enjoyment . . . of all human rights and fundamental freedoms as recognized in the Charter of the United Nations, the Universal Declaration of Human Rights, and international human rights law.

It specifically asserts that Indigenous peoples have the right to self-determination with regard to political status and economic, social, and cultural development. It also states that Indigenous peoples have the right to "autonomy or self-government" in their internal and local affairs and the right to "the ways and means for financing" those functions. In a clear reference to Indigenous peoples' shared history of being forced from their homes by colonizing powers, the Declaration states:

> Indigenous peoples shall not be forcibly removed from their lands or territories. No relocation shall take place without the free, prior and informed consent of the indigenous peoples concerned and after agreement on just and fair compensation and, where possible, with the option of return.

in 1999, titled *Human Rights of Indigenous Peoples: Study on Treaties, Agreements and Other Constructive Arrangements between States and Indigenous Populations.* The report concluded that Indigenous treaty rights in the United States are still effective today. This finding was based largely on Article VI of the US Constitution, which provides that

> all treaties made, or which shall be made, under the Authority of the United States, shall be the supreme Law of the Land; and the Judges in every State shall be

bound thereby, any Thing in the Constitution or Laws of any State to the Contrary notwithstanding.

Article I, Section 8, of the Constitution also explicitly includes relations with Indigenous nations as one of the powers of Congress: "To regulate Commerce with foreign Nations, and among the several States, and with the Indian Tribes." This power remains in effect.

TO DO

The UN study on treaties is a useful tool for Indigenous peoples in the United States in their continuing struggles for land restoration, other treaty rights (such as fishing rights), and sovereignty. As students of history, you also have much to learn from the information in this monumental study. You can find it on the United Nations website, or ask your librarian to help you find a copy.

NATIVE NATIONS IN COURT: INDIGENOUS ACTIVISM IN THE US INTO THE 2010S

Indigenous peoples had learned that US government policies could change, depending on who was in power. Some administrations chose to ignore obligations or delay funds that, by treaty or other legal agreement, were owed to the tribal nations. In the 1980s some Native nations began to use their sovereignty to create sources of revenue that would make the economies of their nations more stable and less dependent on the government honoring its agreements. The creation of the National Indian Gaming Association in 1985 was one such effort. Its purpose is to protect tribal sovereignty and promote the ability of tribes to become more self-sufficient by operating bingo parlors, slot machines, and casinos. By 2015 about half of the federally recognized nations were managing gaming operations that generated more than $25 billion annually. In some nations, tribal citizens receive a per capita payment, like what shareholders in big corporations get. Profits have also been used to develop educational and linguistic programs, to build homes and hospitals, and to invest in larger projects such as the Smithsonian Institution's National Museum of the American Indian.

Some states, however, objected to Indigenous gaming operations. The state of California tried to place limits on winnings at the high-stakes bingo hall the Cabazon Band of Mission Indians started in the early 1980s. The state raided the bingo hall and sued the tribe. The case went to the US Supreme Court in 1987. The court ruled that tribal nations have inherent rights to engage in gambling on their reservations, which means that those fundamental rights cannot be legally taken away. Unhappy with the ruling, several states successfully lobbied Congress to get some of the tribal gaming revenues for state coffers. In 1988 Congress passed the Indian Gaming Regulatory Act (IGRA). IGRA affirmed sovereignty and self-determination for Native nations, but it also gave states the power to place some limits on Indian gaming. Many Native people are concerned that similar court cases have chipped away at the power of Native nations to make all decisions regarding their gaming operations.

The many treaties Indigenous nations negotiated with the United States included transfer of Native lands to the government. But Native land and resources were often taken illegally, outside the terms of treaties. As a result,

The National Museum of the American Indian (NMAI) houses one of the world's largest collections of objects, photographs, archives, and media created by and about Indigenous peoples of the Western Hemisphere. NMAI is located on the National Mall in Washington, DC. Its design incorporates several themes that emerged out of dialogue with Indigenous communities. Its curving lines evoke wind-sculpted rock formations, its front door faces east, the direction of the rising sun, and it has a dome that is open to the sky.

Almost six hundred distinct tribal nations were present for its opening ceremonies on September 21, 2004, and according to the museum's website, it was "the largest known gathering of Native American communities in history."

Native peoples have some legal standing to demand return of their lands.

When a government agrees to compensate a group for something taken from them without their consent, the term often used for this compensation is *reparations*. In 1988, for example, President Ronald Reagan signed a law that provided $20,000 to each Japanese American survivor of the World War II internment camps to compensate them for loss of property and liberty during their internment by the US government. Reparations often come in the form of a monetary payment. Instead of monetary reparations, Indigenous peoples, including those who are legal scholars, demand the return of the lands, water, and other resources that were illegally taken from them, in violation of treaties.

In some cases, the United States has acknowledged that the claims are valid. Sometimes the settlement has involved return of land to the Native nation, as with the return of Blue Lake to Taos Pueblo. Returning land to tribal nations is unpopular with some segments of the non-Native population, however, and the government has chosen to offer monetary compensation instead.

Sioux claims to the Black Hills of South Dakota are a good example. The Sioux tribes first filed suit to regain the Black Hills in 1921. They based their claim on the 1851 and 1868 treaties of Fort Laramie, which established the Great Sioux Reservation. The reservation included the Black Hills, which were sacred to the Sioux people. Much of that land was later taken by acts of Congress, which, as the Sioux people pointed out, violated the terms of the treaty. After decades of legal effort and years of intense protests, the US Supreme Court ruled on July 23, 1980, that the Black Hills had been taken illegally. Instead of restoring the Black Hills to the Sioux people, the court decided that the tribes should be paid nearly $106 million for the land. The Sioux nations refused the payment and continue to demand return of the Black Hills. The money has remained in an interest-bearing account, which by 2010, amounted to more than $757 million. Most Sioux people feel that accepting the money would validate the US theft of their most sacred land.

Thefts of another kind have been going on for hundreds of years. All across the continent Indigenous ruins, graves, and sacred sites have been plundered for research and profit. Anthropologists, archaeologists, artifact dealers, and hobbyists have taken Indigenous artifacts like pottery, arrowheads, and stone tools in addition to human remains, burial items, and other sacred or culturally significant objects. These were put in museums or in private collections, where they could be studied or simply hoarded away from the public. In some places, human remains were displayed as curiosities for tourists. This was usually done without permission from the Native communities and families from which the items were taken. Buying and selling these items became a profitable business, and an underground market flourished. After decades of pressure from tribal governments and individuals, Congress passed the Native American Graves Protection and Repatriation Act of 1990 (NAGPRA). NAGPRA requires museums to return human remains and burial items to their Indigenous communities. It is fitting that Congress used the term *repatriation* in the act. Before NAGPRA, the federal government had used *repatriation* to describe the return of remains of prisoners of war to foreign nations. Native American nations are also sovereign, and Congress correctly characterized the returns as repatriations.

It would take decades of pressure to get the US government to address another major issue: violence against Native women. For many years, calls for justice for Native women who are abused or assaulted have gone unheard. A recent study commissioned by the US Department of Justice found that the rates of domestic abuse and assault against Native women exceed those of any other group in the US, and that the majority of the violent acts are committed by non-Natives.[12] However, prosecution of non-Natives is complicated by legal rules about who has the authority to prosecute non-Natives who commit crimes on Indian reservations: tribes, states, or the federal government. Since the 1970s, tribes could not prosecute non-Indians who committed crimes on their land. Only the federal government could, and often declined to do so. As a result, countless Native women who were abused or assaulted never saw justice done. In 2013, Congress took an important first step toward stopping this violence by allowing tribal nations to prosecute non-Natives for domestic violence and dating violence, as part of its reauthorization of the Violence Against Women Act (VAWA). One Native survivor of domestic abuse commented:

> Now, our tribal officers have jurisdiction for the first time to do something about certain crimes. But it is just the first sliver of the full moon that we need to protect us.[13]

Protection against domestic violence is, indeed, just a sliver of the broader safeguards that are needed to end the violence that many Native women face in their lifetimes. Indigenous advocates view the 2013 changes to VAWA as a move in the right direction, and they continue to lobby Congress to go further by empowering tribal governments to prosecute additional violent crimes against Native women.

■ ■ ■

The work of resistance in the fifty-year period covered in this chapter was carried out by Indigenous elders and youth, with young people in the forefront. With their eyes on sovereignty, they persisted in the face of tremendous opposition. Native people put their bodies on the line time after time, committing civil disobedience and facing down law enforcement. They were sometimes beaten and often arrested, but they were resilient and creative in their pursuit of justice. They reached out to Indigenous peoples around the globe and created alliances to address issues that concerned them all. In the offices of government officials and in the courts, they argued repeatedly for justice for Indigenous communities and nations.

The persistence of the elders and the rising generation raised awareness of Indigenous peoples' concerns at many levels of US society and led to the passage of laws that continue to galvanize and influence the work of Indigenous peoples today. In 2017 this persistence was at the core of a global fight that took place near the Standing Rock Sioux Tribe's reservation. At the heart of that fight was water.

"WATER IS LIFE"

Indigenous Resistance
in the Twenty-First Century

The history of the United States is a story of constant resistance by sovereign Indigenous nations against the forces of settler colonialism. Native peoples steadfastly asserted their sovereignty and their rights to their homelands and the resources there. Even after their losses of the late 1800s, with their populations decimated and in dire poverty, Native people used all available means to protect their religious practices and cultural traditions, to hold on to the land, and to have the US government recognize their sovereignty.

This chapter presents a case study of a relatively recent episode when Indigenous peoples stood against government and private business interests: the 2014–2017 protests against the Dakota Access Pipeline (DAPL) on the Standing Rock Sioux reservation in North Dakota. It begins with some background information and briefly summarizes some key events in the Standing Rock resistance. Then many concepts and issues discussed in earlier chapters are applied to an analysis of what took place at Standing Rock in the twenty-first century.

Background to the Standing Rock Protest

According to the US Department of Energy, an estimated 10 percent of all the energy resources in the United States are on Indian land, even though Indian land is only about 5 percent of the country's total land area.[1] These energy resources include low-sulfur coal, oil, natural gas, and uranium. It is no surprise that the energy industries have often targeted Native land for their mining and drilling operations, which often damage resources essential to the Native communities. Uranium mining and the testing and storage of nuclear weapons and radioactive waste have created hazardous sites that threaten the health of Native and non-Native residents in the western United States. The communities have seldom been fairly compensated for these damages.

The Indian Self-Determination Act of 1975 made it possible for Indigenous nations to have more control over resources on their lands. For some Indigenous nations, greater power to make decisions led to tension between protecting all their resources and using them to generate income. For example, some Navajo people objected when a coal gasification plant was built on tribal land to provide electricity for Phoenix and Los Angeles but very little for the Navajo Nation. Activists also fought for decades against unrestricted strip mining for coal and uranium, the cause of much ecological destruction and deadly health effects in Native communities.

Many communities each year are forced to deal with releases of toxic chemicals into the water, soil, and air. Some of these chemicals can cause lasting harm to a community's water supply, even in small amounts. The damage they cause to the environment is usually permanent. Public pressure sometimes forces polluting companies to clean up after themselves. Even then, the affected communities often find that the polluters do only the bare minimum to restore the environment.

Indigenous governments have used their knowledge of environmental laws and their rights as sovereign nations during conflicts with corporations and government agencies over protection of natural and cultural resources. For example, before building a pipeline, the government and the companies involved must do an environmental impact study to determine how the pipeline and its construction will affect nearby communities. These studies are supposed to look at how a pipeline might affect the soil, air, and water and at the impact it might have on cultural and historical resources such as cemeteries or sacred sites. Specific departments within the United States government, such as the Army Corps of Engineers, and oil companies are required to consult with the tribes during these impact studies. When they do not, Native people have used that failure as the basis for formal complaints or legal action, or as the rallying point for public protest.

Native resistance to TransCanada's Keystone XL (KXL) pipeline project has been a good example of this. Proposed in 2008, that pipeline would carry crude oil from Canada across or near several reservations and directly over the Ogallala Aquifer, a large underground water source essential to millions of people in Nebraska and surrounding states. In general, the government's process of granting permits for KXL overlooked treaty rights and did not meaningfully involve Indigenous nations, even those that would be most affected by the pipeline.

Native nations, non-Native landowners, and environmental activists worked together to fight construction of the KXL. They used a wide range of strategies at the local and national levels, from meeting with decision makers in Washington, DC, to getting arrested on a reservation for blocking trucks carrying pipeline components, to setting up camps near proposed pipeline construction zones. Their vocal and visible resistance raised public awareness of the potential harm from KXL and other pipelines. In January 2012 President Barack Obama rejected the permit for the northern stretch of the KXL that crossed the US border with Canada, saying that the State Department needed more time to collect information about the possible hazards of the proposed pipeline in order to make sure he could "protect the American people."[2] Trans-Canada was allowed to submit another application, and even though construction continued on part of the pipeline in Oklahoma, many consider Obama's rejection an important victory.

The KXL protests brought public attention to both the hazards of pipelines and the importance of organized resistance and civil disobedience. But energy companies continued to plan and build other pipelines. Fewer than two years after the KXL project seemed to have been stopped, Indigenous peoples would launch another pipeline protest that would gain international attention.

Standing with Standing Rock

The Standing Rock Sioux Indian Reservation is the home of Lakota and Dakota people of the Standing Rock Sioux Tribe. Their original homelands include parts of what are currently called the states of North and South Dakota, Wyoming, Montana, Minnesota, Iowa, and Nebraska. The 1851 Treaty of Fort Laramie established a large territory for the Sioux people, but the Treaty of 1868 reduced that land base. In the years after 1868, much more land was taken from the Sioux in violation of the treaty, and the people were left with several much smaller reservations. The Lake Oahe Dam project that began in 1948 destroyed thousands of acres of timber, grazing, and farmland that had belonged to the tribes.

Lake Oahe became a significant source of drinking water for the people of Standing Rock. Then in 2014, an energy company proposed a pipeline that put that water at risk.

Energy Transfer Partners (ETP) proposed the Dakota Access Pipeline (DAPL) to carry hydraulically fractured (fracked) crude oil twelve hundred miles from oil fields in northern North Dakota to existing pipelines in southern Illinois. The ETP website says that the company gathered public input

CONSIDER THIS

When dropping water levels in Lake Oahe exposed remains and cemeteries in 2000, the Standing Rock Sioux joined the Yankton Sioux in a lawsuit under the Native American Graves Protection and Repatriation Act (NAGPRA) to protect the exposed artifacts and remains. Scientists predict that changing climate may cause an increase in droughts and flooding, which means that more sites like the one at Lake Oahe will be exposed. What role do you see for NAGPRA if that happens?

through open houses, meetings, and hearings in four states and made adjustments to the route to avoid environmentally or culturally sensitive areas. One of these adjustments moved it away from Bismarck, the state capital of North Dakota. One early proposal had the pipeline crossing the Missouri River north of the city, but that route was abandoned for one that placed the crossing under Lake Oahe, just north of the Standing Rock Sioux reservation. According to ETP, this route would use less pipe, have fewer water crossings, and be farther from residential water supplies.

The people of the Standing Rock reservation asserted that this route violated terms of the Fort Laramie Treaty and US environmental regulations, and that it put their own residential water supply at risk.

They made these objections clear to pipeline company representatives during a meeting at Standing Rock on

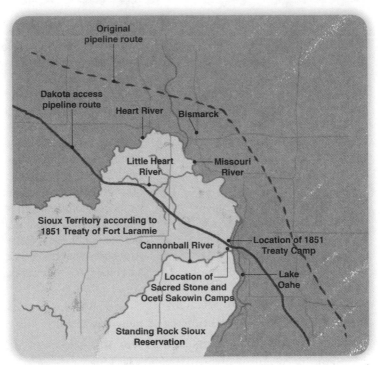

This map depicts many of the places discussed in this chapter, including the early proposed pipeline route north of Bismarck and the lands that belonged to the Sioux according to the 1851 Treaty of Fort Laramie, which the Standing Rock Sioux fought to protect.

September 30, 2014. Tribal Chairman David Archambault told them:

> We have a standing resolution that was passed in 2012 that opposes any pipeline within the treaty boundary. So just so you know coming in, this is something that the tribe is not supporting. This is something the tribe does not wish.[3]

Tribal members also pointed out that the proposed pipeline would cross underneath Lake Oahe, Standing Rock's source of drinking water.

CONSIDER THIS

Government agencies and businesses often make decisions related to environmental quality without much attention to input from the people in the communities that will be the most profoundly affected by polluted air, water, and soil. Research has shown that African American, Latino, or Indigenous communities are far more likely to be close to a landfill, coal-fired power plant, or other source of pollution than white middle-class or wealthy communities. This situation is called *environmental racism*. High-poverty white communities, such as those in mining areas of Appalachia, are also likely to be shut out of decision-making that affects their environment.

In response to these issues, the environmental justice movement works to enable people in any community to fight back against regulations and practices that expose them to environmental hazards. Many people suspected that environmental racism had a role in the decision to move the DAPL away from majority-white Bismarck and closer to the Standing Rock reservation.

Find out where the worst sources of water, air, or soil pollution are in your community. Are they located near areas with high-income or mostly white populations or near those populations that are mainly low income, Indigenous, or people of color?

Tribal Historical Preservation Officer Waste Win Young stated that the tribe was aware that oil companies have often tried to lay pipe in ways that circumvent the National Historic Preservation Act and the National Environmental Protection Act. She also explained the historical and cultural importance of a Dakota village now submerged in Lake Oahe in the path of the pipeline. The village was the site of a massacre by US troops in 1863. Several hundred Sioux families had been hunting and preparing food for the winter. Their leaders included Big Head and Little Soldier. After the soldiers attacked, the survivors crossed the river to escape:

> Chief Big Head's family crossed the water here. When night fell, the babies were crying, and the young girls carried them across the river. They plugged their nose so they wouldn't be heard crying. They swam across the Missouri River with those babies. This is a story that many of us do not know, but it's an important part of our story that needs to be put out there.[4]

Young continued that she had struggled with whether to share the story of the massacre:

> Do we want to tell something that's so important and sacred to us to a pipeline company? But it's important for you guys to know the history and our connection to this area. . . . Today Chief Big Head's descendants are in the room, Chief Little Soldier's, and as well as many of the descendants of a lot of other chiefs. And for us to officially endorse or accept a proposal that would negatively impact our cultural sites, our prayer sites, our duties and responsibilities as stewards of the land . . . goes against the very intent of our office in fighting and protecting and preserving what we have here, what we have left for our people and our children.[5]

In spite of what they learned at the meeting with the Standing Rock tribal council, ETP and the Corps of Engineers proceeded with the DAPL. The company stated that its approval process involved "hundreds of public meetings and thousands of study documents."[6] Few of those meetings and documents, however, involved consultations with the Standing Rock Sioux Tribe, and the tribe never gave approval. ETP published an environmental impact statement in December of 2015 that said the pipeline would not harm tribally significant areas. The tribe disagreed, but ETP continued with their plans to lay the pipeline. The people of Standing Rock, however, made plans to stop them.

On April 1, 2016, LaDonna Brave Bull Allard established Sacred Stone Camp, the first of several that would be set up for people who wanted to join the opposition to the pipeline. The camp was on her family's land where the Cannonball River joins the Missouri River. The name Sacred Stone Camp was inspired by ancient round rock formations created there over thousands of years by a whirlpool. But, Allard says, "the stones are not created anymore, ever since the US Army Corps of Engineers dredged the mouth of the Cannonball River and flooded the area in the late 1950s as they finished the Oahe dam. They killed a portion of our sacred river."[7]

On July 25 the corps authorized the oil company to begin drilling underneath Lake Oahe. Two days later the Standing Rock Sioux Tribe filed an injunction, and the oil company sued the chairman for blocking construction. Over the coming months lawyers for the tribe and the company appeared in courtrooms many times as the tribe fought the pipeline. Early in August, Archambault, Tribal Councilman Dana Yellow Fat, Alayna Eagle Shield, and several other people were arrested while attempting to approach a construction site. Eagle Shield was working for the tribe as a language specialist. A few days after her arrest, she began looking for people with traditional knowledge who could help her provide schooling for the children whose parents were in the camps. Shortly after that she started Mní Wičhóni Nakíčižiŋ Owáyawa, the Defenders of the Water School.

By August 2016 several thousand people, including writers, attorneys, and medical personnel, were living in the camps, collectively called Oceti Sakowin (Seven Fires). The population included members of over one hundred Indigenous nations of North, Central, and South America, as well as South Africa, Norway, and the Philippines. Because the people who gathered at Standing Rock were there to protect the water, they called themselves "Water Protectors." The pipeline company, law enforcement, and the news media usually called them "protesters," which emphasized objection to the pipeline rather than the goal of saving the region's water supply.

While some who came to Standing Rock stayed for many months, many of them went to lend support for a few days or weeks. Most of the people were there to resist through prayer and nonviolent action.

From the start, however, many local residents wanted the Morton County sheriff to stop the Water Protectors. The townspeople and local law enforcement frequently mischaracterized some nonviolent protest actions like roadblocks as "violent." On social media and in some newspaper comment sections, they used disparaging and stereotypical ways of talking about Indigenous peoples in the camps.

On August 19 the governor of North Dakota declared a state of emergency for southwest and south-central North Dakota. It allowed him and the Morton County

When they weren't in classes, children at the Standing Rock camps found places to play, as children did during the occupation of Alcatraz Island nearly forty years earlier.

sheriff to mobilize a military-type response to these non-violent protests, while saying publicly that the right to protest is constitutionally protected. This move pleased many non-Native local residents who were disturbed by the presence of so many protestors. National Guard troops and law enforcement officers from other states eventually became part of a months-long standoff with the Water Protectors. They set up checkpoints and road-blocks where officers checked travelers' ID and questioned them about where they were going and what they planned to do. They began frequent air surveillance of the camps, using small planes and helicopters.

News outlets and social media played important roles in getting the attention of a national and international audience. Indigenous peoples effectively used social media to attract the interest of the press and to communicate with people far away from the protests. With cameras attached to drones, they made videos that provided a compelling visual record of what was happening. Some broadcast "live" using Facebook's live video streaming option. On Twitter and Facebook, they used hashtags like #NoDAPL and #WaterIsLife to inform the public. The Water Protectors also allowed a journalist from the news program *Democracy Now!* to report from Standing Rock. The news and social media coverage generated great concern among people who were following the events there. They expressed their support through donations of money, goods, and legal services; by taking part in demonstrations at banks that funded the pipeline; and by joining marches like the Rise with Standing Rock march in Washington, DC, on March 10, 2017.

Celebrities such as actors Shailene Woodley and Mark Ruffalo joined the Water Protectors at the camps. Their presence drew greater media attention. Many people around the world were shocked to see a September 3 video of dogs attacking Water Protectors who tried to stand in front of machinery that was digging to lay more pipeline. The dogs belonged to a security firm hired by the Dakota Access Pipeline company. Footage filmed and broadcast by *Democracy Now!* showed the security guards letting the dogs off leash and encouraging them to attack the protectors, some of whom were on horses. These attacks prompted Chairman Archambault to ask the Department of Justice to investigate policing and apparent violations of civil rights at Standing Rock.

On October 23 some Water Protectors set up a new camp directly in the path of the pipeline, on Cannonball Ranch land that ETP had recently purchased. Though the ranch was not part of the reservation, it was on land

Militarized law enforcement used a variety of weapons at Standing Rock and dressed as if ready for battle, in camouflage and riot gear. The large light colored military vehicle on the road in this photo appears to have an LRAD (long range acoustic device) Sound Cannon mounted on its roof.

that the Lakota people regard as theirs, based on terms of the 1851 Treaty of Fort Laramie. This "1851 Treaty Camp" had about fifteen tipis and fifty tents. On October 27 police and National Guard in riot gear and Humvees closed in on the camp. They used tear gas, batons, rubber bullets, and "sound cannons," which emit painfully loud blasts, and they arrested more than one hundred people. They also arranged a vehicle blockade at Backwater Bridge on the main road through the area. Someone later set those vehicles on fire. Some sources blamed protesters, but others said that security company employees set the fires.

Law enforcement continued to block the bridge after the October 27 raid, adding concrete barriers and concertina wire to the barricade. This made it difficult for Water Protectors to get to the drilling site. It also forced people at the camps to take a much longer route to town, and it blocked emergency vehicles going to and from the camps. Even area residents who were not part of the protest were affected by the blockade. Before long it became a highly visible flashpoint.

In early November, videos circulated on social media of forty or fifty young people, Native, white, and black, trying to make their way across the Cannonball River to a burial ground. Wrapped in Mylar blankets, they held hands and prayed as they crossed through the forty-degree waist-high water. Law enforcement officers in riot gear were lined up on the riverbank to stop them. The young people asked the police to leave the burial grounds. Filmmaker Josh Fox was observing the interactions between the two groups. He heard the young people say, "All we want is clean water." But before long, Fox reported, a teen was taken away in an ambulance, shot by an officer at close range with a rubber bullet. Fox talked with several young people who had been pepper-sprayed. Later, he saw another journalist get shot with a rubber bullet. Reflecting on what he witnessed at Standing Rock, Fox wrote:

> It is as if American history is being played out in miniature. On one side, the terrible legacy of the genocidal Indian wars of Manifest Destiny, atrocity, and slaughter. On the other side, the great American tradition of equality, egalitarianism, the Bill of Rights, democracy, the fight for human rights. The collision course of history couldn't be clearer than it is at Standing Rock.

On one side, the descendants both genealogically and ideologically of General Custer and on the other side, Sitting Bull, Crazy Horse, and Wounded Knee. The ghosts of history dance in front of us on the water. The vapors of tear gas and pepper spray menacing their legacy. It is the fight for the climate, for the Bill of Rights, and for all of America standing there shivering in the water.[8]

On November 20, news and social media reported about a nighttime confrontation on the Backwater Bridge. That night Water Protectors began to remove the burned vehicles that law enforcement was using as barricades on the bridge. On the other side of the blockade were law enforcement and security personnel, many wearing riot gear. The sheriff's office stated that protesters aggressively attacked the police in the process of trying to dismantle the barricade, but video footage does not support that claim. The police fired tear gas and concussion grenades, injuring many. Water Protectors built some small fires to keep warm, as temperatures were well below freezing that night. The police called the fires a safety issue and directed high-power water hoses at the fires and at the people. By the time the confrontation ended, over two hundred protectors had been treated for hypothermia and minor injuries. Several others were hospitalized for more serious injuries, including a woman whose arm was blown apart by a rubber bullet and elders who had been teargassed.

As winter and heavy snow set in, some protectors left, but many others stayed. Groups of US military veterans numbering about two thousand arrived to support those

Holding their "Water Is Life" or "Defend the Sacred" signs,
Water Protectors stand behind a barricade across the highway.

who remained in the camps. Stunned by news reports, many veterans planned to stand as human shields between law enforcement and Water Protectors. The Standing Rock Sioux Tribe and others affected by the pipeline continued their fights in court, at Standing Rock, at banks that funded the pipeline, and at sporting events that provided high visibility.

Over the next six months there were several seemingly significant wins. Shortly after the events at Backwater Bridge, the tribe called on President Obama to deny the pipeline company the easement it needed and to protect tribal sovereignty. The easement was not granted, and the Corps of Engineers began to prepare environmental impact statements for other possible routes.

Some setbacks followed. The result of the 2016 presidential election was especially damaging to the

At sports arenas around the country, Water Protectors hung banners like this one to call on US banks to stop investing in the Dakota Access Pipeline.

resistance. The Republican president-elect was an investor in one of the companies that owned a stake in the Dakota Access Pipeline project. On January 24, 2017, his administration authorized a go-ahead on the drilling at Lake Oahe. On June 1 the pipeline was put into service. In December, current Standing Rock Tribal Chair Mike Faith said that the DAPL remained a danger to the people of Standing Rock and should be shut down. He said the tribe was gratified that the Corps of Engineers and DAPL must now include the tribe in emergency response planning and the company must file regular reports on pipeline incidents or repairs.

It remains to be seen whether the corps and the pipeline company will follow the court's order. As previous chapters have demonstrated, history is full of examples of court decisions and treaties being twisted to the disadvantage of Indigenous peoples or ignored outright.

Indigenous resistance to the Dakota Access Pipeline is one of the most significant moments in the history of Indigenous peoples of the United States. Events there are echoes of earlier periods in history, but those historical periods themselves foreshadowed what happened at Standing Rock. This part of the chapter analyzes how some of those echoes of the past were present in the Standing Rock protest:

- Indigenous sovereignty
- Indigenous peoples' care for the land and resources
- the Doctrine of Discovery
- the history of treaties broken by the United States,
- Indigenous resistance to being colonized
- militarized response to Indigenous resistance
- the role of mass media in public perceptions of Indigenous resistance
- use of the US legal system to protect Indigenous rights
- mistaken ideas and stereotypes of Indigenous peoples

The exercise of sovereignty was at the core of Native resistance to the Dakota Access Pipeline. You have read that hundreds of distinct sovereign nations thrived on this continent for thousands of years before Europeans arrived here. These sovereign nations had complex interactions, engaging in trade, diplomacy, and sometimes forming alliances in times of war. You have also read that the people cared for each other and their communities through wise use of the continent's natural resources—land, water, plants, and animals. They knew that safe water for drinking, cleansing, and irrigation was essential to life. Responsibility for protecting it was passed down from one generation to the next.

Sovereignty and the protection of vital resources came together at Standing Rock. The Standing Rock Sioux Tribe's resistance to the Dakota Access Pipeline was necessary because the Army Corps of Engineers and the pipeline company did not acknowledge and respect the tribe's sovereign authority to determine what happens to its resources (in this case, water) and its sacred sites. From the elders to the infant born at the camp, the peoples of many sovereign Native nations gathered to support the Standing Rock Sioux Tribe. As one people, they declared that land and resources are not commodities that can be bought and sold for individual or corporate profit. Instead, these resources sustain life and should be used respectfully, for the benefit of all. From the letters leaders of many nations wrote to the signs people carried, all proclaimed "Water Is Life." And so, they fought the Dakota Access Pipeline.

In earlier chapters you read about the Doctrine of Discovery, a set of laws issued by the Vatican beginning in 1452 that enabled European powers to justify conquest and exploitation of lands that did not belong to them. All European nations came to rely on this doctrine, which, in their minds, bestowed on them a God-given right to colonize the homelands of other peoples. For centuries it provided legal cover for genocide and the theft of Indigenous lands and resources. Though most US laws do not mention the Doctrine of Discovery, its idea is so present in the minds of so many people that they don't realize it is shaping their attitudes and actions. It enables people in corporations and government agencies to justify doing what they want to do with Indigenous lands and resources in places like Standing Rock. Indigenous peoples have fought against it from the start. Other non-Native groups have also recognized the injustice. That occurred at Standing Rock when a group of non-Native clergy denounced the Doctrine of Discovery and took the provocative step of burning copies of it to demonstrate their understanding of its harm.

In December 2016 the Standing Rock, Cheyenne River, and Yankton Sioux Tribes appealed for help to the Inter-American Commission on Human Rights. Tribal representatives were invited to testify at the commission's hearings on the impact of extraction industry projects such as mining and pipeline construction on Indigenous peoples' human rights. The final report on the hearings makes clear that actions against the Standing Rock Water Protectors by government agencies, the pipeline company, and law enforcement were not unique to the United States.

The historical failure of the United States to abide by its treaties with the Sioux was also a factor in the resistance at Standing Rock. Article VI of the US Constitution says that "All Treaties made, or which shall be made, under the Authority of the United States, shall be the supreme Law of the Land." And yet Congress took away large sections of the reservation that had been promised to the Sioux forever. The Standing Rock Sioux referred to the original treaties of Fort Laramie to make the case that the pipeline company and the Corps of Engineers were ignoring the tribe's land rights.

The people at Standing Rock repeatedly expressed their commitment to stopping the pipeline through peaceful action. They did not want weapons in the camps. The response to their resistance was militarized alliance among local police, the National Guard, and the pipeline company's private security forces that deployed military vehicles and weapons against the Water Protectors. This response was familiar to the people gathered there. For hundreds of years Europeans and then Americans turned away from diplomacy with Native peoples. If they couldn't quickly get what they wanted through negotiations, they called in militias or the army. The colonizers quickly became comfortable with waging war against women, children, and elders and found ways to excuse what they did, such as claiming that Indigenous peoples were not using "civilized" ways of war.

Law enforcement at Standing Rock clearly saw themselves as defending the pipeline company from an enemy. Their public statements consistently described the protests as threatening, even when the participants had been praying or singing. The local sheriff's office even referred to the Native people as doing "war whoops" and "counting coup," which sounded a lot like the way people in the 1800s talked about "frontier" warfare in "Indian country."

DEFINITION

The term *counting coup* was first used by French soldiers, and later British and US soldiers, to describe a technique used by Native fighters during warfare. It refers to getting close enough to an enemy to touch or strike with the hand or a weapon held in the hand, which required courage beyond what was needed to kill someone from afar. Each nation had terms in its own language for such actions.

When the protesters became assertive by building Treaty Camp directly in the pipeline path or wading across the river to reach a burial ground, law enforcement, often wearing riot gear, justified attacking them with pepper spray, sonic weapons, rubber bullets, and water cannons. When private security guards released attack dogs, the police did not intervene. Law enforcement at Standing Rock was always more heavily armed and armored than any of the Water Protectors.

The nonviolent resistance at Standing Rock and the militarized response drew attention from the national news media. In the 1800s, news reports had generated sympathy and respect for the Nez Perce, Modoc, and other nations who were at war with the US military. One key difference between Standing Rock and those earlier events is that this time the Native people themselves were able to record and report what was going on. They could get information directly to allies outside the camps and allowed reporters into the camps to help them reach a wider audience.

Standing Rock's legal teams used the US legal system, as many tribal nations did before them, to fight business interests and the government in court. Then as now, the courts delivered wins and losses. Standing Rock's resistance to the pipeline is another example of a Native nation affirming its sovereign status in court, asserting its right to self-determination, and standing up for its economic and political best interests. The numbers of Native and non-Native attorneys and people who are well versed in laws that affect Indigenous communities have grown tremendously since the 1800s. They have formed coalitions and use environmental laws, treaties, land rights, and the media to fight the US government and anyone else who infringes on the rights of Indigenous nations.

The Standing Rock resistance was especially effective at interrupting stereotypes and mistaken ideas about Indigenous peoples that have infected the minds of non-Native people since the 1400s. Indigenous peoples were not "wiped out" by colonization. They were not "savage," incompetent, lazy, or primitive creatures. Instead, the world witnessed Indigenous communities united in purpose. They weren't "drunken Indians" or defeated warriors at the end of the trail. They were lawyers, writers, and orators, children and elders, spiritual and governmental leaders all committed to nonviolence with confidence in their goal: to protect the water by asserting Native sovereignty.

What happened at Standing Rock is not unique. Again and again, businesses have used the US military to get access to the Indigenous peoples' land and resources they wanted and to protect their interests once they got what they wanted. Again and again, agreements were made and broken by the United States in ways that were helpful to business interests. Again and again, Indigenous peoples stood against them. Many historians point out a similar pattern in how the US deals with less powerful nations around the world when US businesses want to use their resources. Its strategies include refusing to meet with local Indigenous leaders to hear how a community may be affected or ignoring their input completely. Sometimes the strategies are military. The US often sends aid, arms, or "advisors" to governments that hope to profit from the presence of US businesses. Those governments then use those resources to suppress dissent when communities protest harm done by the actions of the US corporations.

Native historian Jack Forbes argues that while living persons are not responsible for what their ancestors did, they are responsible for the society they live in, which is a product of that past. As you've read through this book, you've seen many instances in which a country that sees itself as exceptional did not behave in exceptional ways. You learned a lot about the ways that Indigenous peoples view their encounters with colonizers.

What does that mean, for you?

You can turn your knowledge into direct action in situations that affect the lives of Native people. If a movie or book misrepresents Native people, you can let others know. Tell your friends. Write to the publisher. Write a movie or book review on social media pointing out the problems you see. You can find out about the issues that Native people face today by following Indigenous media such as *Indian Country Today* and *Native America Calling,* and by following social media conversations that use hashtags like #NativeTwitter. Inform yourself about those

CONSIDER THIS

Many people who cared about what happened at Standing Rock wanted to be physically present at a historic moment when people stood together against injustice. But many made a wise choice not to go to the resistance camps. Showing up at Standing Rock was a good option for people who could pay for their own travel, who brought food and supplies to share, and who were prepared for the possible challenges such as being cold or getting arrested. Other kinds of support were also critically important. For example, many people took part in demonstrations against the pipeline in Washington, DC, and other places around the country. Many supporters sent warm clothes and other supplies to the camps, and thousands donated money to cover expenses such as legal fees for Water Protectors who were arrested. Others wrote supportive letters to media outlets, their congresspersons, or the president. Or they offered solid information on social media to counter rumors and lies about Standing Rock. Protests continue throughout the United States. Before going to them, think about how you will be most effective.

issues and take some time to figure out how you might be the most helpful.

■ ■ ■

Pipeline construction, mining, and other forms of exploitation are sure to continue in the twenty-first century. Native people will persist in protecting their communities, their lands, their water, their sacred sites, and the wider world from the risks.

Knowing how to be in that future world is your challenge.

In this young people's adaptation of *An Indigenous Peoples' History of the United States,* you may have noticed that there is more information about Indigenous men than Indigenous women. That imbalance is the result of history being written by men who chose to write about men. Below are the names of Indigenous women. You'll recognize two, because those two appear frequently in histories and biographies: Sacajawea and Pocahontas. Both women are significant, but it is important to seek out Indigenous writers when looking for information about them. Most books about them have been written by non-Native people who replicate errors about them. You're fortunate that we live in a period of increasing attention to historical accuracy. We encourage you to learn about the women named in the list below, which includes politicians, professors, performers, doctors, writers, artists, and lawyers. What other Native women would you add?

Irene Bedard	Winona LaDuke
Tantoo Cardinal	Lozen
Brenda Child	Wilma Mankiller
Elizabeth Cook-Lynn	Maria Martinez
Louise Erdrich	Beatrice Medicine
Deb Haaland	Deborah Miranda
Joy Harjo	Rebecca Nagle
Suzan Shown Harjo	Nora Naranjo-Morse
Diane Humetewa	Elizabeth Peratrovich
Betty Mae Tiger Jumper	Susan La Flesche Picotte

Pocahontas

Christine Quintasket

Marcie Rendon

Sacagawea

Buffy Sainte-Marie

Shoni Schimmel

Joanne Shenandoah

Cynthia Leitich Smith

Arigon Starr

Roxanne Swentzell

Maria Tallchief

Toypurina

Haunani-Kay Trask

Annie Dodge Wauneka

Sarah Winnemucca

Ofelia Zepeda

Zitkála-Šá

SOME BOOKS WE RECOMMEND

By now you have probably read many picture books, chapter books, and novels that have Native characters or themes—books like *Island of the Blue Dolphins* or *Little House on the Prairie*. Many of them, however, are by non-Native writers and illustrators. They contain errors, bias, and stereotypes, and they're set in the past. Though they may be award-winning or classics, the information in them is wrong, and we are pleased when teachers and librarians decide to set them aside and use books by Native writers instead. We hope you will look for the books we list below, to read yourself or to share with others. Though this book, *An Indigenous Peoples' History of the United States for Young People*, is meant for young adult readers, we are including picture books in our list because they are not, in fact, "just for little kids." There is much to learn from all the books we list on the next page!

All the books listed below are by Indigenous writers. When you tell others about them, tell them the author's name and that author's nation! To get that information, you will have to do some research. Find the author's website or biography in the book, and you'll find the name of the nation. Then you can say, "Hey, check out Art Coulson's book about Jim Thorpe! Coulson is Cherokee. Thorpe played football at one of those racist Indian boarding schools and was such a good athlete that he won a bunch of Olympic gold medals." Or you could hand them *Hearts Unbroken* and say, "The author, Cynthia Leitich Smith, is Muscogee. Her book is partly about a Native kid trying to figure out if he wants to be the Tin Man in the school play. Did you know L. Frank Baum—that guy who wrote *The Wizard of Oz*—wanted to kill off all the Native Americans?"

Annie Boochever with Roy Peratrovich Jr. *Fighter in Velvet Gloves: Alaska Civil Rights Hero Elizabeth Peratrovich*. Fairbanks: University of Alaska Press/Snowy Owl Books, 2019.

Joseph Bruchac. *Hidden Roots*. New York: Scholastic, 2004.

Lisa Charleyboy and Mary Beth Leatherdale, editors. *Dreaming in Indian: Contemporary Native American Voices*. Toronto: Annick Press, 2014.

Lisa Charleyboy and Mary Beth Leatherdale, editors. *#NotYourPrincess: Voices of Native American Women*. Toronto: Annick Press, 2017.

Brenda J. Child, Gordon Jourdain, and Jonathan Thunder. *Bowwow Powwow*. St. Paul: Minnesota Historical Society, 2018.

Art Coulson and Nick Hardcastle. *Unstoppable: How Jim Thorpe and the Carlisle Indian School Football Team Defeated Army*. North Mankato, MN: Capstone Editions, 2018.

Heid Erdrich, editor. *New Poets of Native Nations*. Minneapolis: Graywolf Press, 2018.

Heid Erdrich, *Original Local: Indigenous Foods, Stories, and Recipes from the Upper Midwest*. St. Paul: Minnesota Historical Society Press, 2013.

Louise Erdrich. *The Birchbark House*. New York: Hyperion Books for Children, 1999. See additional titles in the series.

Louise Erdrich. *The Round House*. New York: Harper Perennial, 2013.

Eric Gansworth. *If I Ever Get Out of Here*. New York: Arthur A. Levine, 2015.

Eric Gansworth. *Give Me Some Truth*. New York: Arthur A. Levine, 2018.

John B. Herrington. *Mission to Space*. Ada, OK: White Dog Press, 2016.

Joseph Marshall III. *In the Footsteps of Crazy Horse*. New York: Amulet Books, 2015.

Carla Messinger. *When the Shadbush Blooms*. Berkeley: Tricycle Press, 2007.

Cheryl Minnema and Wesley Ballinger. *Hungry Johnny*. St. Paul: Minnesota Historical Society Press, 2014.

Jonathan Nelson, *The Wool of Jonesy*. Albuquerque: Native Realities, 2016.

Hope Nicholson, editor. *Love Beyond Body, Space, and Time: An Indigenous LGBT Sci-Fi Anthology*. Winnipeg: Bedside Press, 2016.

Hope Nicholson and Michael A. Sheyahshe, editors. *Moonshot: The Indigenous Comics Collection*, volume I. Toronto: AH Comics, 2015. See also volume II.

Simon J. Ortiz and Sharol Graves. *The People Shall Continue*. New York: Lee and Low Press, 2017.

Anita Poleahla and Emmet Navakuku, *Celebrate My Hopi Corn*. Flagstaff: Salina Bookshelf, 2016.

Marcie Rendon. *Murder on the Red River*. El Paso: Cinco Puntos Press, 2017.

Joanne Robertson. *The Water Walker*. Toronto: Second Story Press, 2017.

Robbie Robertson and David Shannon. *Hiawatha and the Peacemaker*. New York: Abrams, 2015.

Sebastian Robertson and Adam Gustavson. *Rock & Roll Highway: The Robbie Robertson Story*. New York: Henry Holt, 2014.

Gary Robinson. *Son Who Returns*. Summertown, TN: 7th Generation, 2014.

Sean Sherman. *The Sioux Chef's Indigenous Kitchen*. Minneapolis: University of Minnesota Press, 2017.

Cynthia Leitich Smith. *Jingle Dancer*. New York: Morrow Junior Books, 2000.

Cynthia Leitich Smith. *Rain Is Not My Indian Name*. New York: HarperCollins, 2001.

Cynthia Leitich Smith. *Indian Shoes*. New York: HarperCollins, 2002.

Cynthia Leitich Smith. *Hearts Unbroken.* Somerville, MA: Candlewick, 2018.

Virginia Driving Hawk Sneve. *The Christmas Coat: Memories of My Sioux Childhood.* New York: Holiday House, 2011.

Traci Sorell and Frané Lessac. *We Are Grateful/Otsaliheliga.* Watertown, MA: Charlesbridge, 2018.

Arigon Starr, editor. *Tales of the Mighty Code Talkers.* Albuquerque: Native Realities, 2016.

Arigon Starr. *Super Indian.* West Hollywood: Wacky Productions, 2012.

Tim Tingle and Karen Clarkson. *Saltypie: A Choctaw Journey from Darkness into Light.* El Paso: Cinco Puntos Press, 2010.

Tim Tingle. *How I Became a Ghost: A Choctaw Trail of Tears Story.* Oklahoma City: Roadrunner Press, 2013.

Tim Tingle. *When a Ghost Talks, Listen: A Choctaw Trail of Tears Story.* Oklahoma City: Roadrunner Press, 2018.

Laura Tohe. *Code Talker Stories.* Tucson: Rio Nuevo Publishers, 2012.

Aslan Tudor and Kelly Tudor. *Young Water Protectors: A Story About Standing Rock.* Calgary: Eaglespeaker Publishing, 2018.

Donald Uluadluak and Qin Leng. *Kamik: An Inuit Puppy Story.* Chicago: Inhabit Media, 2013.

Daniel Vandever. *Fall in Line, Holden!* Flagstaff: Salina Bookshelf, 2017.

NOTES

Introduction: This Land

1. Patrick Wolfe, "Settler Colonialism and the Elimination of the Native," *Journal of Genocide Research* 8, no. 4 (December 2006): 387.

2. Thomas Jefferson, *The Writings of Thomas Jefferson,* ed. Andrew Adgate Lipscomb, Albert Ellery Bergh, and Richard Holland Johnson (Washington, DC: Thomas Jefferson Memorial Association of the United States, 1907), 296.

3. Walter R. Echo-Hawk, *In the Courts of the Conqueror: The 10 Worst Indian Law Cases Ever Decided* (Golden, CO: Fulcrum, 2010), 77–78.

4. "Genocide," UN Office on Genocide Prevention and the Responsibility to Protect, http://www.un.org/en/genocide prevention/genocide.html, accessed November 27, 2018.

5. John F. Marszalek, *Sherman: A Soldier's Passion for Order* (New York: Free Press, 1992), 379.

6. Jean M. O'Brien, *Firsting and Lasting: Writing Indians Out of Existence in New England* (Minneapolis: University of Minnesota Press, 2010).

Chapter One: Follow the Corn

1. "Peacekeeping Traditions of the Iroquois Confederacy," *Peace Talks* (radio), November 25, 2005, http://www.goodradio shows.org/peaceTalksL33.html.

2. Emmet Starr, *History of the Cherokee Indians and Their Legends and Folk Lore* (Oklahoma City: Warden, 1921), 22.

Chapter Two: Culture of Conquest

1. Francis Jennings, *The Invasion of America: Indians, Colonialism, and the Cant of Conquest* (New York: W. W. Norton, 1976), 168.

Chapter Three: Cult of the Covenant

1. John Mack Faragher, Mary Jo Buhle, Daniel H. Czitrom, and Susan Armitage, *Out of Many: A History of the American People,* vol. 1, 8th ed. (New York: Pearson, 2015), 1.

2. Jennings, *The Invasion of America,* 15.

3. "Naturalization Oath of Allegiance to the United States of America," US Citizenship and Immigration Services website, https://www.uscis.gov/us-citizenship/naturalization-test /naturalization-oath-allegiance-united-states-america, accessed October 13, 2018.

4. Billy Kennedy, *Our Most Priceless Heritage: The Lasting Legacy of the Scots-Irish in America* (Greenville, SC: Ambassador International, 2005).

Chapter Four: Bloody Footprints

1. John Grenier, *The First Way of War: American War Making on the Frontier, 1607–1814* (Cambridge, UK: Cambridge University Press, 2008), 6.

2. John W. Shy, "A New Look at Colonial Militia," *William and Mary Quarterly* 20, no. 2 (1963): 175–85.

3. Grenier, *The First Way of War,* 42.

4. Colin G. Calloway, *The Scratch of a Pen: 1763 and the Transformation of North America* (New York: Oxford University Press, 2006), 73.

5. Grenier, *The First Way of War,* 29.

6. Grenier, *The First Way of War,* 69.

7. Colin G. Calloway, *The American Revolution in Indian Country: Crisis and Diversity in Native American Communities* (Cambridge, UK: Cambridge University Press, 1995), 197.

8. Grenier, *The First Way of War,* 18.

9. Alexander Martin, "Instructions to Charles McDowell Concerning an Expedition Against the Cherokee Nation," July 23, 1782, Colonial and State Records of North Carolina 16: 697–98, Documenting the American South, University of North Carolina at Chapel Hill website, https://docsouth.unc.edu/csr /index.html/document/csr16-0489, accessed October 19, 2018.

10. "To George Washington from the Seneca Chiefs, 1 December 1790," Founders Online, https://founders.archives.gov /documents/Washington/05-07-02-0005, accessed October 13, 2018.

11. Reuben Gold Thwaites and Louise Phelps Kellogg, *Documentary History of Dunmore's War*, 1774 (Madison: Wisconsin Historical Society, 1905), 86.

12. Laws of the United States of America from the 4th of March, 1789, to the 4th of March, 1815, vol. 1 (Philadelphia: John Bioren and W. John Duane), 605.

13. Daniel Richter, *Facing East from Indian Country: A Native History of Early America* (Cambridge, MA: Harvard University Press, 2001), 74.

14. Richter, *Facing East from Indian Country*, 223

15. Richard Drinnon, *Facing West: The Metaphysics of Indian-Hating and Empire Building* (Minneapolis: University of Minnesota Press, 1980), 331.

Chapter Five: The Birth of a Nation

1. Raymond J. DeMallie and Vine Deloria Jr., *Documents of American Indian Diplomacy: Treaties, Agreements, and Conventions*, vol. 1, 1775–1979 (Norman: University of Oklahoma Press, 1999).

2. Grenier, *The First Way of War*, 195.

3. Michael D. Green, *The Politics of Indian Removal: Creek Government and Society in Crisis* (Lincoln: University of Nebraska Press, 1982), 26.

4. Grenier, *The First Way of War*, 176.

5. Grenier, *The First Way of War*, 177.

6. Grenier, *The First Way of War*, 187.

Chapter Six: Jefferson, Jackson, and the Pursuit of Indigenous Homelands

1. Boutros Boutros-Ghali, Interim Report of the Commission of Experts Established Pursuant to Security Council Resolution 780 (January 1993), 16. https://undocs.org/S/25274, accessed December 13, 2018.

2. Boutros Boutros-Ghali, Final Report of the Commission of Experts Established Pursuant to Security Council Resolution 780 (May 1994), 33. https://undocs.org/S/1994/674, accessed December 13, 2018.

3. "From Thomas Jefferson to William Henry Harrison, 27 February 1803," Founders Online, https://founders.archives.gov/documents/Jefferson/01-39-02-0500, accessed February 11, 2019.

4. Grenier, *The First Way of War*, 204.

5. James M. Mooney, *Historical Sketch of the Cherokee* (1900) (Chicago: Aldine Transacter, 1975), 124.

6. Alexis de Tocqueville, *Democracy in America*, trans. Henry Reeve (New York: Colonial Press, 1900; originally published in 1838), 113.

Chapter Seven: Sea to Shining Sea

1. George E. Tinker, *Missionary Conquest: The Gospel and Native American Cultural Genocide* (Minneapolis: Fortress Press, 1993), 42.

2. Wai-chee Dimock, *Empire for Liberty: Melville and the Poetics of Individualism* (Princeton, NJ: Princeton University Press, 1989), 9.

3. John Reynolds, *John Brown, Abolitionist: The Man Who Killed Slavery, Sparked the Civil War, and Seeded Civil Rights* (New York: Vintage, 2005), 449.

4. Reginald Horsman, *Race and Manifest Destiny: The Origins of American Racial Anglo-Saxonism* (Cambridge: MA: Harvard University Press, 1981), 235.

5. Robert W. Johannsen, *To the Halls of the Montezumas: The Mexican War in the American Imagination* (New York: Oxford University Press, 1988), 218.

Chapter Eight: Indigenous Lands Become "Indian Country"

1. Alice Marriott and Carol K. Rachlin, *American Indian Mythology* (New York: Thomas Y. Crowell, 1968), 139.

2. United States War Department, *Report of the Secretary of War, Being Part of the Message and Documents Communicated to the Two Houses of Congress at the Beginning of the Second Session of the Fifty-Second Congress*, vol. 1 (Washington, DC: Government Printing Office, 1892), 219.

3. United States Department of the Interior, *Report of the Secretary of the Interior Being Part of the Message and Documents Communicated to the Two Houses of Congress at the Beginning of the First Session of the Forty-Fourth Congress*, vol. 1 (Washington, DC: Government Printing Office, 1875), 366.

4. Robert G. Hays, *A Race at Bay: New York Times Editorials on "The Indian Problem," 1860–1900* (Carbondale: Southern Illinois University Press, 1997), 10.

5. *Official Report of the Nineteenth Annual Conference of Charities and Correction* (1892), 46–59, quoted in Richard H. Pratt, "The Advantages of Mingling Indians with Whites," *Americanizing the American Indians: Writings by the "Friends of the Indian," 1880–1900* (Cambridge, MA: Harvard University Press, 1973), 260–71.

Chapter Nine: The Persistence of Sovereignty

1. Edwin R. Embree, *Indians of the Americas* (Boston: Houghton Mifflin, 1939), 226.

2. Yvonne Leif, "Boarding Schools for Indian Children," interview, *All Things Considered,* National Public Radio, October 14, 1991.

3. Maria Shaa Tláa Williams, ed., *The Alaska Native Reader: History, Culture, Politics* (Durham, NC: Duke University Press, 2009), 1.

4. Joe S. Sando, *Pueblo Nations: Eight Centuries of Pueblo Indian History* (Santa Fe, NM: Clear Light, 1992), 117.

5. Lisa Brooks, "Intellectual History," in *The Oxford Handbook of American Indian History*, ed. Frederick E. Hoxie (New York: Oxford University Press, 2016), 528.

6. Matthew L. M. Fletcher, *Federal Indian Law* (St. Paul: West Academic Publishing, 2016).

7. Richard Drinnon, *Keeper of the Concentration Camps: Dillon S. Myer and American Racism* (Berkeley: University of California Press, 1987), 235.

Chapter Ten: Indigenous Action, Indigenous Rights

1. Daniel M. Cobb, *Native Activism in Cold War America: The Struggle for Sovereignty* (Lawrence: University of Kansas Press, 2010), 52.

2. Cobb, *Native Activism in Cold War America*, 60.

3. David E. Wilkins, ed., *The Hank Adams Reader: An Exemplary Native Activist and the Unleashing of Indigenous Sovereignty* (Golden, CO: Fulcrum, 2011), 179.

4. Howard Zinn, *A People's History of the United States, 1492–Present* (New York: HarperCollins, 1995), 526–27.

5. United States v. Washington, 384 F. Supp 312 at 28 (W.D. Wash. 1974), https://wdfw.wa.gov/fishing/salmon/BoldtDecision8.5x11layoutforweb.pdf , accessed December 16, 2018.

6. Troy Johnson, "The Occupation of Alcatraz Island: Roots of American Indian Activism," *Wičazo Ša Review* 10, no. 2 (Autumn 1994): 63–79.

7. Donna Hightower Langston, "American Indian Women's Activism in the 1960s and 1970s," *Hypatia* 18, no. 2 (Spring 2003): 118.

8. Susan Lobo, ed., *Urban Voices: The Bay Area American Indian Community* (Tucson: University of Arizona Press, 2002), 80.

9. Truman Lowe, James Luna, and Paul Chaat Smith, *James Luna: Emendatio* (Washington, DC: National Museum of the American Indian, 2005), 32.

10. Fletcher, *Federal Indian Law*, 422.

11. Vine Deloria Jr., *Behind the Trail of Broken Treaties: An Indian Declaration of Independence* (Austin: University of Texas Press, 1985), 78.

12. André B. Rosay, *Violence Against American and Alaska Native Women and Men: 2010 Findings from the National Intimate Partner and Sexual Violence Survey* (Washington, DC: US Department of Justice, May 2016), https://www.ncjrs.gov/pdffiles1/nij/249736.pdf.

13. Sari Horwitz, "New Law Offers Protection to Abused Native American Women," *Washington Post*, February 8, 2014, http://wapo.st/NmaOqq?tid=ss_tw&utm_term=.eca2704cba88.

Conclusion: "Water Is Life"

1. Lizana K. Pierce, *DOE's Tribal Energy Program* (Washington, DC: US Department of Energy, 2016), https://www.energy.gov/sites/prod/files/2016/01/f28/0811review_01pierce.pdf.

2. Barack Obama, "Statement by the President on the Keystone XK Pipeline," White House Office of the Press Secretary, January 18, 2012, https://obamawhitehouse.archives.gov/the-press-office/2012/01/18/statement-president-keystone-xl-pipeline.

3. "September 30th DAPL Meeting with SRST," transcription of audio recording, 4, EarthJustice.org, https://earthjustice.org/sites/default/files/files/Ex6-J-Hasselman-Decl.pdf, accessed October 13, 2018.

4. "September 30th DAPL Meeting with SRST," 15.

5. "September 30th DAPL Meeting with SRST," 16–17.

6. Dakota Access Pipeline Facts, "What Was the Regulatory Process for Approving the Dakota Access Pipeline?," https://daplpipelinefacts.com/dt_articles/what-was-regulatory-process-for-approving-dakota-access-pipeline/, accessed December 14, 2018.

7. LaDonna Brave Bull Allard, "Why the Founder of Standing Rock Sioux Camp Can't Forget the Whitestone Massacre," *Yes Magazine*, September 3, 2016, https://www.yesmagazine.org/people-power/why-the-founder-of-standing-rock-sioux-camp-cant-forget-the-whitestone-massacre-20160903.

8. Josh Fox, "Shot in the Back at Standing Rock," *Daily Beast*, November 14, 2016, https://www.thedailybeast.com/shot-in-the-back-at-standing-rock.

9. Jenni Monet, "Standing Rock Joins the World's Indigenous Fighting for Land and Life," *Yes Magazine*, September 30, 2016, https://www.yesmagazine.org/people-power/standing-rock-joins-the-worlds-indigenous-fighting-for-land-and-life-20160930.

IMAGE CREDITS

PG. 113   This drawing of the wall was made by Roy S. Dickens in 1979 for *Archaeological Investigations at Horseshoe Bend.*

PG. 125   Courtesy of the Architect of the Capitol, 2011.

PG. 141   Allen Memorial Art Museum, Oberlin College, Ohio; gift of Mrs. Jacob D. Cox, 1904.

PG. 142   Courtesy of Artful Doodlers

PG. 144   Courtesy of the Library of Congress, Prints and Photographs Division, 1890.

PG. 145   Courtesy of the US Geological Survey.

PG. 147   Courtesy of the National Parks Service, 1870s.

PG. 148   Courtesy of the Library of Congress, Prints and Photographs Division. Photograph by Frank A. Rinehart, 1898.

PG. 152   Courtesy of *New York Tribune*, 1877.

PG. 156   Courtesy of the US Department of the Interior, 1911.

PG. 160   Carlisle Indian School, photograph by Francis Benjamin Johnston, 1901.

PG. 160   Carlisle Indian School, photograph by Francis Benjamin Johnston, 1901.

PG. 161   Courtesy of the Library of Congress, Prints and Photographs Division.

PG. 162   Courtesy of the US Department of the Interior, 1912.

PG. 166   *Ko Hawaii Pae Aina*, 1878.

PG. 167   *Hawaii's Story by Hawaii's Queen, Liliuokalani,* 1898.

PG. 168   From the collection of Gertrude Svarny; photograph by Charles H. Hope, her father.

PG. 176   Courtesy of the Library of Congress, Prints and Photographs Division. Photograph by Warren K. Leffler, 1978.

PG. 179   Larry Dion/*Seattle Times*.

PG. 180   Photo: © Dolores Varela Phillips Collection. University of Washington Libraries, Special Collections, UW 39992.

PG. 182   Copyright © 2019 by Ilka Hartmann. www.ilkahartmann.com

PG. 183   AP Photo.

PG. 184 Courtesy of the Bancroft Library, Berkeley, CA.
PG. 188 Bettmann/Getty.
PG. 190 Courtesy of the Library of Congress, Prints and Photographs Division. Poster by Bruce Carter, 1970.
PG. 197 Courtesy of the Smithsonian Institution.
PG. 208 Courtesy of Artful Doodlers
PG. 213 Courtesy of Angus Mordant.
PG. 215 Courtesy of Camille Seaman.
PG. 218 Courtesy of Camille Seaman.
PG. 219 Carlos Gonzalez, copyright 2017, *Star Tribune.*
PG. 222 Courtesy of Camille Seaman.

INDEX

This index is different from the indexes you see in other books. In parentheses following the names of individuals, we provide information about each person's identity, such as the Native nation or citizenship in a country. For example, George Washington was of European ancestry, born in a British colony in North America, and became a citizen of the United States of America after it was formed. So the index entry for him is "Washington, George (Euro-American, US)." The entry for a Native leader such as David Archambault includes his nation: Archambault, David (Standing Rock Sioux Tribe). We do this to emphasize that everybody's origins are important.

NOTE: Page numbers in *bold italics* indicate illustrations

destroy the Navajo, 142; impact on Indigenous people, 137–38

Clarke, Elijah (Euro-American, US), 104

client class: defined, 101; and forced indebtedness, 110–11, 123–24

Cobell v. Salazar class-action lawsuit, 204

Collier, John (Euro-American, US), 172

colonization, European: defined, 5–6; as a divine entitlement, 44, 51–52, 62–63; importance of Indigenous infrastructure, 29, 49; and land ownership, 34–35, 60–61; and the myth of the virgin wilderness, 49–50; role of surveyors/speculators, 81; and the term "America," 3. *See also* Doctrine of Discovery; genocide; origin stories/myths

Colorado Volunteers, Sand Creek Massacre, 140–41

Columbus, Christopher (Italy), 4–5, 43

Comanches: homelands, 106, 123, 125; resistance efforts, 126, 136–37; Santa Fe Trail, 130–31

the commons, 34–35

community, Indigenous emphasis on, 26, 28, 175, 190

Connecticut, colony of, Pequot opposition to, 72

conquistadors, 43

Continental Congress: and the efforts to destroy the Shawnee Nation, 82; Northwest Ordinance, 6

Cooper, James Fenimore (Euro-American, US), 133

corn: cultivation and distribution, 18–19, 26; Indigenous terms for, 18; and the Three Sisters story, 20; transcontinental trade and traditions, 29–30

Cortez (Spain), 23

Cottier, Belva (Sioux), 182, *182*

counting coup, defined, 224

covenant with God, as the justification for colonization, 48, 51–56, 59–60, 62–63. *See also* Doctrine of Discovery; Manifest Destiny

Crazy Horse (Oglala Lakota), 151

Crow Creek Sioux Reservation, exile of Dakota to, 140

Crow people, 106, 170

the Crusades, 33–34, 37

Culhua peoples, 21–22

cult, defined, 47

Curtis Act (1898), 155

Custer, George Armstrong (Euro-American, US): defeat by the Sioux and Cheyenne at the Battle of the Greasy Grass, 151; military actions west of the Mississippi, 143;

scientific expedition into the Black Hills, 150

Custer Died for Your Sins (Deloria), 193

Dakota Access Pipeline (DAPL) project: nonviolent protests, 31, 202–3, 207, 211–18, *219*, 221, 227; Oceti Sakowin (Seven Fires) camps, 212, *213*; proposal for, 207–8, *208*; violent responses to protests, 212–17, 223–25; the Water Protectors, 214–18, *215*, *218*, 221, *221*

Dakota peoples, 139–40, 150. *See also* Dakota Access Pipeline (DAPL) project; Sioux Nation

Darwin, Charles (England), 41

Dawes Act (1887), 154–55

Declaration of Independence, 52–53

Declaration of Indian Purpose (1961), 177

Deganawidah-Quetzalcoatl University, 186

Delaware (Lenape) Nation: homelands, 78–79, *79*; massacre of, 83–84; pacifism, 82–83; resistance by, 93

Delaware, colony of, Indigenous homelands in, 79

Deloria, Vine, Jr. (Standing Rock Sioux), 88–89, 193

DeMallie, Raymond J. (Euro-American, US), 88–89

Democracy Now! 214

dependency, policies promoting, 44, 110–11, 117, 123–24

The Discovery, Settlement and Present State of Kentucke (Filson), 133–34

DNA analysis, limits of, 38–39

Doctrine of Discovery: assumption of white supremacy and entitlement, 49, 81, 123, 222; role of the Catholic pope, 4, 33, 43

domestic violence, 199–200

Dominican Republic, 43

Dragging Canoe (Cherokee), 102

Dunmore, Earl of (John Murray) (England), 80

Eagle Shield, Alayna (Standing Rock Sioux), 211–12

Echo-Hawk, Walter R. (Pawnee), 10

"1851 Treaty Camp," 215

Eisenhower, Dwight D. (Euro-American, US), 174

ekvnv vnoksulke ("people greedily grasping after the land"), 98

El Camino Real, 127

Embree, Edwin (Euro-American, US), 161–63

Emerson, Ralph Waldo (Euro-American, US), 135

Endecott, John (England), 72–73

End of the Trail (Fraser), *14*

Lakota Sioux: Battle of the Greasy Grass (1876), 151; and the Black Hills, 150; Ghost Dance, 153; homelands, 206, 214–15; occupation of the BIA building, *188*; word for buffalo, 146

Landing of Columbus (Vanderlyn), *5*

land ownership: and the Alaskan gold rush, 168–69; allotment policies, 154–55; 158; and the idea of private property, 34–36, 60; as the idea underlying colonialism, 2–6, 12–13, 104–5; and expansionism/Manifest Destiny, 8–10, 80–81, 106, 110–11, 132, 157; and the Lincoln administration, 137; and poverty, 41–42, 45; and US national parks/"public use" areas, 169–70. *See also* reservations; treaties; *specific nations and peoples*

land stewardship, Indigenous: and the buffalo, 144–45; and efforts to regain stolen land, 197–98; as focus, 31; and habitat management, 27–28; Indigenous lands, extent of before 1500, 10–11, *12*; and road systems, 28–29; and serving the common good, 60. See also *specific nations and peoples*

languages, Indigenous, 97–98

lawsuits: *Cobell v. Salazar*, 204; and fishing rights, 181; against Georgia, by the Cherokee Nation, 115–16; and the Indian Claims Commission, 173; and reparations, 197–98. *See also* Dakota Access Pipeline (DAPL) project

Leatherstocking Tales (Cooper), 133

ledger illustrations, *141*

Liliuokalani (queen of Hawai'i), 167, *167*

limpieza de sangre ("cleanliness of blood"), 37

Lincoln, Abraham (Euro-American, US): approval of execution of Dakota men, 139–40; and the elimination of Indigenous peoples from the West, 140; Gettysburg Address, 53; support for thefts of Indigenous lands, 137

Little Soldier (Yankton Dakota), 210

The Lone Ranger, 66

Longest Walk event, Washington, DC, *176*

Long Walk, *142*

Lord Dunmore's War, 80–81

Louisiana Purchase, 106, *107*

Lowell, James Russell (Euro-American, US), 135

Lower Creeks, economic dependence, 111–12

Lyons, Oren (Onondaga), 26

Mackay, Hugh, Jr. (Scotland), 74
mahiz (corn), 18
Makah Nation, fishing
grounds, 179
mandaamin (corn), 18
Manifest Destiny: atrocities
associated with, 216; as
inevitable, God's will, 8–9;
multicultural interpreta-
tion, 9–10; as part of the
US origin myth, 135
Martinez, Esther (Ohkay
Owingeh), 98
Martinez, Lorenzo (Taos
Pueblo), 162–63
Maskoke language (Mus-
cogee), 97–98
Mason, John (England), 72–73
Massachusetts Bay Colony,
51, 52
massacres: Battle of Horse-
shoe Bend, 112–13; at
Gnadenhutten, 83–84;
at Sand Creek, 140–41;
at the village under Lake
Oahe, 209–10; by the Vol-
unteer Army of the Pacific,
141–42; at Wounded Knee
Creek, 153–54
Mathews, George (Euro-
American, US), 104
Mayan civilization, 21–22, 97
Mayflower Compact, 51, 53
McGillivray, Alexander (Mus-
cogee), 101–2
McIntosh, Lachlan (Scotland),
82
Means, Russell (Oglala La-
kota), 189

Menominee Nation, Wiscon-
sin, 174
mercenaries: attack on the
Powhatans, 70; attacks
on the Pequots, 73; and
attacks on the Red Sticks,
112; defined, 70; rangers,
65–66, 74–75; and settle-
ment of the Ohio frontier,
91–92. See also militias
Meshekinnoqquah (Little
Turtle, Miami), 91–92
Mesoamerica, 18, 21, 29
Mexico: the Aztecs, 22–23;
casta painting from,
38–39, 39; flight of
Indigenous peoples to,
129; independence, 126,
128–29; land grant sys-
tem, 130–32; northern,
US colonization of, 126,
129–30; the Olmecs, 22;
policies related to enslavement, 131; trading with
the US government, 130;
US war with, 131–32,
134–35
Miami Nation, 92–93
Michigan, Indigenous homelands in, 7
militarism: and colonization,
59–60, 223–24; defined,
56; and regular vs. irregular warfare, 64, 63
militias: colonial, 65; defined,
65; at the Ohio frontier,
92, 105; and the Ulster
Scots, 56. See also mercenaries; rangers

Mills, Sid (Yakima and Cherokee), 180
Minisota Makoce (Land Where the Waters Reflect the Skies or Heavens), 139
Minnesota: Indigenous activism in, 181; Indigenous homelands in, 7, 106, 206; statehood, 139
Mirabel, Porfirio (Taos Pueblo), 162
Miranda, Lin-Manuel (Latinx/Puerto Rican, US), 86
missionaries: in California, 127; government financial support for, 159; among the Kanaka Maoli, *166*; in New Spain, 123–24; treatment of Indigenous captives, 124–25, 127–28. *See also* boarding schools; Doctrine of Discovery
Mission San Antonio de Valero, 126
Mississippi River: and the French and Indian War, 76; and Indigenous homelands, 30; Mississippi Valley city-states, 24; as a trade route, 107
Mní Wičhóni Nakíčižiŋ Owáyawa (Defenders of the Water School), 212
Modocs, Modoc War, 149–50, 225
Mohawk Nation, 25, 84–85. *See also* Haudenosaunee Confederacy

Monet, Jenni (Laguna Pueblo), 223
Monkman, William Kent (Cree), *6*
Monks Mound, 25
Monroe, James (Euro-American, US), 115, 121
Mooney, James (Euro-American, US), 119
Moravian Protestants, 82–83
Morrill Act (1862), 137
Morton County, North Dakota, and the DAPL protests, 212–16, 224–25
mound builder civilizations, 24
Muckleshoot Indian Tribe, Treaty Trek, *179*
Musogee Creek Nation: alliances and resistance, 101; during the Civil War, 138; conflicts between the Upper and Lower Creeks, 111–12; homelands, 24, 96; Maskoke language, 97–98; militia attacks on, 101–4; origins in Mexico, 29–30; removal, 120; Treaty of New York, 100
Muslims: and Christian white supremacy, 36–37; and the Crusades, 33–34; genocide against, 40–41
Myer, Dillon S. (Euro-American, US), 174

Nambé Pueblo, seed pot from, *30*
Natchez Nation, 24

182–85; Indigenous population, 181–82
Santa Fe Trail, 130–31
Sauk Nation, 118
scalping, scalp hunters, 56, 66–67, 75, 77–78, 86, 92, 141
Scotch-Irish. *See* Ulster Scots
Seagrove, George (Euro-American, US), 102–4
Sealth (Chief Seattle; Suquamish and Duwamis), 163
seed pots, *30*
self-determination. *See* sovereignty
Seminole Nation: during the Civil War, 138; removal to Oklahoma, 1832, 115, 120; survival as a nation, 115
Seminole Wars (1817–1819), 115
Seneca Nation: affiliation with the British, 85; in the Haudenosaunee Confederacy, 25; name given to George Washington, 81
Sequoyah (Cherokee), syllabary, 98
Serra, Junipero (Spain), 127–28
"settler," as a term, 5
settler colonialism, 11–15
Settler War for Independence from Britain: and British efforts to recruit Cherokees, 76; Muscogee neutrality during, 96; role of Ulster Scot soldiers, 59

Seven Years War, 68
Sevier, John (Euro-American, US), 99, 102–3
sexual abuse: and domestic violence, 199–200; in Indian Schools, 164
Shawnee Nation: alliance with the British, 81; alliance with the Red Sticks, 112; efforts to destroy, 82; homelands, 78–79, *79*; ranger attacks on, 80; resistance by, 93–94; theft of hunting grounds, 80
Sherman, William Tecumseh (Euro-American, US): and the buffalo slaughter, 146; genocide by, 13; military actions west of the Mississippi, 143
Shoshone people, 141, 170
Shy, John W. (Euro-American, US), 65
Sioux Nation: and the Black Hills, 150, 198; defensive alliances, 146–47; Great Sioux Reservation, 150, 198; violence at Pine Ridge, 189. *See also* Dakota Access Pipeline (DAPL) project; Standing Rock Sioux, Standing Rock Sioux Reservation, North Dakota
Sitting Bull (Hunkpapa Lakota), 151–53
Six Nations of the Iroquois Confederacy. *See* Haudenosaunee Confederacy

smallpox, 71
Smith, John (England), 65, 69
Snake tribes, 149
social media: stereotyping and, 212; as tool for activism, 18, 213–14, 217–18, 227
sovereignty: Apache, and POW status, 148; and the DAPL protests, 220; and gaming, 195–96; Hawaiian, 166–67; and the Indian Reorganization Act, 172–73; and the New Deal, 172–73; and the Ohio Country, 91; struggles to retain or regain, 158, 174, 176–77, 181, 187, 190–92, 201, 220; Termination Era, 174; and the UN study on treaties, 194–95. *See also* Dakota Access Pipeline (DAPL) project; treaties; *specific nations and peoples*
Spain: conflicts with the British, 75; conquests of Indigenous peoples, 4, 123–25; desire for gold, 43; Doctrine of Discovery, 4, 43, 49, 81, 123, 222; land claims in North America, 43, 122–23; protection of missions, 128; settlements in the Texas area, 126; Spanish Florida, 96, 115
sports teams, names given, 66
squatters: defined, 58; efforts to provoke wars, 100;

Muscogee name for, 98; in the Ohio Country, 93–94, 96; US government support, 99
"squaw," as a term, viii
Standing Rock Sioux, Standing Rock Sioux Reservation, North Dakota: relocation to, 206; resistance, 203–6, 224–25, 227; Sacred Stone Camp, 211; and violations of treaty rights, 223. *See also* Dakota Access Pipeline (DAPL) project; Water Protectors, Standing Rock
Starr, Emmet (Cherokee), 29–30
statehood, requirements for, 135
Stephenson, Matilda Coxe (Euro-American, US), 162
stereotyping: approaches to ending, 227–28; of Indigenous peoples, 36, 39, *39*, 52, 222; newspapers and, 151–52; societal treatment of "the other," 33; of Standing Rock protesters, 212, 220, 225
stewardship, defined, 27
Sullivan, John (Euro-American, US), 85
"Sun Elk," 161–63
surveyors, 80–81, 109, 131–32
Survival of American Indians Association, 179–80
symbols, 97

ROXANNE DUNBAR-ORTIZ is a historian, author, memoirist, and speaker who researches Western Hemisphere history and international human rights. She grew up in rural Oklahoma and lives in San Francisco. She has been active in the international Indigenous movement for more than four decades and is known for her lifelong commitment to national and international social justice issues. After receiving her PhD in history at the University of California at Los Angeles, she taught in the newly established Native American Studies Program at California State University, Hayward, and helped found the Departments of Ethnic Studies and Women's Studies. Her first book, *The Great Sioux Nation*, was the fundamental document at the first international conference on Indigenous peoples of the Americas, held in 1977, at the United Nations' headquarters in Geneva. Dunbar-Ortiz is the author or editor of twelve other books, including *Roots of Resistance: A History of Land Tenure in New Mexico*, *"All the Real Indians Died Off": And 20 Other Myths About Native Americans*, *Loaded: A Disarming History of the Second Amendment*, and the memoir, *Red Dirt: Growing Up Okie*.

JEAN MENDOZA holds a PhD in curriculum and instruction and an MEd in early childhood education from the University of Illinois at Urbana-Champaign.

DEBBIE REESE is an educator and founder of American Indians in Children's Literature (AICL). She is tribally enrolled at Nambé Owingeh, a federally recognized tribe, and grew up on Nambé's reservation. She holds a PhD in Curriculum and Instruction from the University of Illinois Urbana-Champaign.